Shepherds and Bathrobes

*To my mother and father, who,
as the best of their many gifts,
taught me the gospel.*

Shepherds and Bathrobes

THOMAS G. LONG

SERMONS FOR ADVENT, CHRISTMAS AND EPIPHANY

(SUNDAYS IN ORDINARY TIME)

CYCLE B GOSPEL TEXTS

C.S.S. Publishing Co., Inc.

Lima, Ohio

Library of Congress Cataloging-in-Publication Data

Long, Thomas G., 1946-
    Shepherds and bathrobes.

    (Cycle B gospel texts)
    1. Church year sermons.   2. Sermons, American.   3. Bible. N.T.
Gospels — Sermons.   I. Title.   II. Series.
BV4253.L66   1987   252'.61   87-8038
ISBN 0-89536-869-2

Table of Contents

6

[1]Common Lectionary
[2]Lutheran Lectionary
[3]Roman Catholic Lectionary

Foreword

Playwright Herb Gardner once described a dream he keeps having. He is seated on a theater stage, frantically scribbling on a pad. On the other side of the drawn curtain can be heard the rustlings and coughings of an audience gathering. The stage manager is nervously pacing, repeatedly glancing at Gardner, who continues to write furiously. It is opening night, and the play is not finished.

Every preacher recognizes this dream and can tell his or her version of it. It is Sunday morning, the congregation settles into the pews after the final stanza of the sermon hymn, all eyes are on the pulpit, an air of electric quietness fills the sanctuary with anticipation . . . and the sermon is not finished.

Whatever psychological value such preachers' dreams carry, they also point to a truth about sermons: they are *never* finished. There is always something else, something more, which can be said, should be said, but the time for preaching has arrived, and frail and incomplete thoughts must fill that deep cavern so innocently labeled "The Sermon." The broken labors of our hands and minds must now be trusted to the continuing sustenance of the Spirit and the faithful care of those who hear. This, then, is a collection of unfinished sermons. I am willing to let them go only because of the hope that, as they are read, they will become more finished in the reader's mind than they are in mine.

All of the sermons in this collection are based upon biblical texts, specifically the gospel passages appearing in the most often-used lectionaries for Advent, Christmas, and Epiphany, Year B. In every case, a serious attempt was made to listen to the text. Some of these texts were frustratingly silent, and, like Jacob wrestling the angel, I had to cling to them, begging for a blessing. Other passages were eager to speak, often saying more than I could retain and always more than I could understand.

These sermons represent a wide variety of styles and methods. This variety is a result, not of stylistic playfulness, but rather from an attempt to let the tone and substance of the texts govern the shapes of the sermons. One additional factor influenced composition. I was aware that these sermons would be *read,* rather than *heard,* and they are, therefore, written for the "eye" rather than for the "ear."

Because of this, they are not, I suppose, actually sermons at all, since preaching is at home only in orality. If, however, they are read by ministers and teachers who find in them some small help for their own task of announcing the good news, then I will be content in the knowledge that these sermons have found their way home.

Thomas G. Long
Princeton, New Jersey

When Something is About to Happen

"I'll tell you what keeps me coming to this church." The man who spoke was punching the air with his finger, pronouncing every word with force, and the dozen or so other people in the room turned to listen. The group called themselves the "Searchers Class," and had done so since the time, more than ten years before, when, as young adults, they had formed an alternative church school class, and "Searchers" had seemed then like a daring and accurate name. Now, as the "Searchers" crept into middle age, the act of searching itself seemed to take more and more energy. Indeed, the whole business of being a part of the church at all felt, at times, like a burdensome weight, and on this Sunday morning that weight had tugged the conversation toward the question, Why stay in the church?

"I'll tell you," he said, "what keeps me coming to this church," and every head turned in his direction. The sudden rush of interest made him hesitate, uncertain of his own thought, but he pushed on. "It's strange, I know, but I get the feeling here, like nowhere else, that something is about to happen."

The feeling that something is about to happen. A strange notion, and yet, the earliest Christians would have recognized it instantly as one of the truest marks of the church. They were convinced they stood on the precipice of history, and that something, indeed, was about to happen. For the world, time lumbered on, day after wearisome day, moving toward who knows what, but, for the early Christian community, something was about to happen. As time crept forward, a great, though yet unseen, future had stirred and gathered itself, and now was sweeping toward time itself on a course of inevitable collision. Something was about to happen.

What was about to happen? Their attempts to describe it strained the boundaries of their language as surely as they strain our contemporary imaginations. "The kingdom of God is at hand . . . The stars will fall from heaven . . . The night is far gone . . . They will see the Son of man coming in clouds with great power and glory . . . This age is passing away . . . Come, Lord Jesus." The church lived on tiptoe, straining their eyes toward the horizon. Something was about to happen.

Because something was about to happen, every word they uttered, every deed they did, every prayer they prayed was shaped by this coming event. Like an actor in a play whose role seems insignificant until the denouement discloses that his lines held the key to the truth all along, the early Christians risked the shame of the world, confidently awaiting the final act.

We have all known, in small ways, the energy an eagerly anticipated future can give to our actions in the present. The expectant parents who find joy in what would otherwise be toil: assembling the crib, painting the nursery, practicing the pushing and the breathing. The residents of a town who mow the lawns, sweep the sidewalks, repair the cracked windows at city hall, and stretch colorful bunting across the store fronts as they ready themselves for the visit of a dignitary. Christmas itself has this kind of power. People brave crowds at the mall and edgy clerks; gifts are carefully chosen, packages wrapped, and ceramic nativity scenes dusted and set, piece by piece, on the mantle. Every action has meaning, because something is about to happen.

But we have also known the sense of loss and disappointment

over a hoped-for future which does not come, when nothing, nothing really, happens. The husband and wife who try to conceive a child, in vain. Or again, plans are changed; the dignitary travels by another route, by-passing the town, leaving the once-festive bunting to droop in the rain. Even Christmas day has its own measure of disappointment. The packages are opened, the gifts admired and put away. The tree comes down; the shepherds and angels are stored for another year, and the long-awaited day passes with a sense that nothing, nothing really, has happened.

In a far more profound way, the church has always struggled with its pain over a future which fails to come. "Come, Lord Jesus," they prayed, but it was Roman soldiers who came. "This world is passing away," they sang, but the world remained. One can live on tiptoe just so long, before the muscles grow tired and the eyes grow weary of looking for the light of a day which never dawns. If the church is standing at the threshold of God's future kingdom of justice, then the church can dare to touch the wounds of lepers and freely pour out its resources for the poor. If this world is surely in the throes of death, and the new age of healing and mercy is close at hand, then the church can cheerfully bear rejection, endure suffering, and faithfully sing its alleluias. But if there is no God-shaped future at hand, if nothing, nothing really, is about to happen, then there is only one more day to be endured in an endless string of days, a bottomless pit of human need, and a ceaseless line of the poor, who are always with us. All there is left for the church to be is another well-meaning institution, and all there is left for the church to do is to whistle its liturgy in the dark, collect the pledge cards and keep the mimeograph machines humming. Because nothing is about to happen.

Even the second generation of Christians, the ones to whom the New Testament was originally addressed, were not immune to this loss of faith in the coming kingdom of God. In the beginning a passionate hope kept the line taut between their present experience and God's future, but as the days wore on and the suffering became intense, and the living memories of Jesus faded, and the world rolled on as before, the tension in the line slackened. The Apostle Paul once captured the vibrant anticipation of those early days when he said, "The appointed time has grown very short." But, as one New Testament scholar observed, gradually the time grew "very long."

It was not despite this, but, to the contrary, *because* of this that the church preserved and repeated the urgency of Jesus' warning, "Take heed, watch, for you do not know when the time will come." (Mark 13:33) No one warns the night watchman to "Stay awake!" unless he appears to be getting drowsy. Just so, the church kept Jesus' call to watchfulness alive in their memory and in their worship, not because they had no problem with hope, but precisely because they *did* have difficulty hoping.

But even a warning from the lips of Jesus cannot keep us vigilant, expectant, and hopeful forever. To be blunt, we cannot "take heed and watch," no matter who told us to do it, when nothing ever happens. The writer of Mark undoubtedly knew this, and that is why, when he wrote these words, he recorded two other words of Jesus as well.

The first is simply this: "Of that day or that hour no one knows, not even the angels in heaven, nor the Son, but only the Father." (Mark 13:32) What this means, starkly put, is that God's future will not arrive when we want it, plan it, or even think we need it. It will come, not according to our timetable, but in its own good time, in God's own good time. The coming kingdom is a promise, and, Hal Lindsey's *The Late Great Planet Earth* notwithstanding, it cannot be turned into a set of predictions, which we can then manipulate. The coming kingdom is a promise from God, and it cannot be domesticated into a political agenda or reduced to the doctrine of progress. God does not provide happy endings for the futures we are engineering. God provides a future beyond our knowledge and control, and not even the angels in heaven know the hour of its coming.

But even with this caution against wanting to know too much, we are still left with too little. We still have the question of how to hope in the meantime, when nothing ever happens. And that is why the writer of Mark remembered the other word which Jesus said. This word was a story, a parable actually, about a man who went on a trip and left his servants to manage the house while he was gone. That, of course, is a description of the situation of the church, left in charge of the house while the Master is absent. What Jesus said about the servants is true also of the church: They need constantly to be on the lookout. The house can never be in disarray, because, as Jesus stated it, "You do not know when the master of the house will come, in the evening, or at midnight, or at cockcrow, or in the morning — lest he come suddenly and find you asleep." (Mark 13:35-36)

Now, at first glance, Jesus seems merely to be saying again, in story form, "of that day or hour no one knows," but the author of Mark hears something different, something more, in this word. The master could come "in the evening," and, in the very next chapter, he tells us that "when it was evening" Jesus ate his last meal with the disciples, and tells them, "one of you will betray me."

Or the master could come "at midnight," and Mark records that, later that night, the disciples went with Jesus to Gethsemane. While Jesus prayed his cry of anguish, the disciples, no doubt weary of waiting, slept. "Could you not watch one hour?" he said to them.

Perhaps the master will come "at cockcrow," and Peter turned to the accusing maid with a curse and a denial, "I do not know this man." The cock crowed.

Maybe the coming of the master will be "in the morning," and "as soon as it was morning," Jesus was bound and led away to his trial and to his death.

What the author of Mark has heard in Jesus' story, and has woven into the fabric of his gospel, is that every moment of the passing day is already alive with the promise of God's future. As the church strains its sight toward the horizon of the coming kingdom, it also hears the ticking of the clock on the wall, and knows that each passing minute is filled with the potential for faith or denial, decision or tragedy, hope or despair. Those who trust in the promise of God's coming kingdom are also able to see advance signs of its coming all around them. Those who believe that, in God's good time, something is about to happen, also know that, even now, something *is* happening. The passing minutes of every day are, like iron filings drawn and aligned toward an unseen magnet, already shaped by God's future and filled with its force.

"I get the feeling here, like nowhere else," mused the man in the Searcher's Class, "that something is about to happen." He said, perhaps, more than he knew. We sometimes lose sight of the fact that every moment of the church's life is formed by the expectation that something is about to happen, and this *something* has to do with God's coming in power to the world. Every time Christians recite the old phrase in the creed, "He will come to judge the quick and the dead," we disclose our hope that frail human justice, the kind one can get with a good lawyer and a full checkbook, is not all the justice life holds. Come, Lord Jesus. Every time some congregation creates a clothing closet or a food pantry for those in need. they do so not because they are so naive as to think that a few used garments and a shelf of soup and cereal are going to end human need. They do so because they live today in the light of God's tomorrow, when all will be clothed in garments of light and the banquet table of the kingdom will hold a feast. Come, Lord Jesus. Every time Christian people speak words of forgiveness in circumstances of bitterness, words of love in situations of hatred, they are speaking in the future present tense. That is, they are using in the present a language which the whole creation will learn to speak in God's tomorrow. Come, Lord Jesus. Every time worshippers struggle to their feet to sing, "Come Thou Long-Expected Jesus, Born to Set Thy People Free," they are praying for, expecting, something to happen, some *one* to happen. Come, Lord Jesus.

Prayer, too, is grounded in the hope that something is about to happen. There is a Hasidic story about a devout man who worked in a slaughter house. His work required him to utter a prayer for mercy before killing each beast. Every morning he said a tearful farewell to his family before leaving for the slaughterhouse, because he was persuaded that his ritual prayer led him into great danger. He feared that, after he called upon God, God might forcefully and devastatingly come to him before he could finish the prayer with, "Have mercy."[1] A harsh truth, but a truth nonetheless. All prayer is based on the confident hope that something is about to happen.

I once taught a confirmation class to a very small group. In fact, there were only three young girls in the class. In one session, I was instructing them about the festivals and seasons of the Christian year, and when we came to the discussion of Pentecost, I asked them if they knew what Pentecost was. Since none of the three knew, I proceeded to inform them that Pentecost was "when the church was sitting in group and the Holy Spirit landed on them like tongues of fire on their heads. Then they spoke the gospel in all the languages of the world." Two of the girls took this information in stride, but the third looked astonished, her eyes wide. I looked back at her, and finally she said, "Gosh, Reverend Long, we must have been absent that Sunday." The beauty of that moment was not that she misunderstood about Pentecost, but that she understood about the church. In her mind, there was the possibility that the event of Pentecost could have happened, even in our Sunday service. "I get the feeling here, like nowhere else, that something is about to happen." Come, Lord Jesus.

And it was the Lord, himself, who said, "What I say to you I say to all. Watch." (Mark 13:37)

Notes

[1] A version of this story appears in Annie Dillard, *Teaching a Stone to Talk,* (New York: Harper and Row, 1982), p. 41.

What Do You Mean, "Repent"?

Bright Lights, Big City is Jay McInerney's searingly-witty, emotion-ripping novel of one young man's perilous drift down an alcohol and white-powder-polluted stream of delayed adolescence. The young man is bright, creative, and desperately lonely. His language is marked by the kind of sarcasm which forms at the intersection of keen intelligence, comic conceit, and human desolation. (He describes a woman he meets as having a voice "like the New Jersey state Anthem played through an electric razor.") Barely holding on to his low-level job at a New York City magazine, he spends most of his time playing with casual relationships in strobe-lit Manhattan bars, wandering through graffiti-scarred scenes of urban decay, and finding his personality to be unraveling at an increasing velocity.

At one point in the novel, the young man, riding an uptown subway and trailing behind him the wreckage of a marriage, a career, and possibly a life, finds himself seated next to a Talmud-reading Hasidic Jew. Watching this Hasid move his finger across the lines of Hebrew, the young man observes,

> *This man has a God and a History, a Community . . . Wearing black wool all summer must seem like a small price to pay. He believes he is one of God's chosen, whereas you feel like an integer in a random series of numbers. Still, what a . . . haircut.*[1]

A God and a History, a Community . . . but what a hair-cut. In some ways, that comes close to the reaction of contemporary people to John the Baptizer, an amalgam of awesome piety and just plain weirdness. He strides into the opening scene of the Gospel of Mark, inevitably bringing with him, for the modern reader, his Hollywood-shaped image. Out of Central Casting, by way of Wardrobe, John stands there with his tumbleweed hairdo, animal skins draped over his outsized frame, popping honey-dipped locusts as his rough baritone howls like the desert wind to the gathering crowds, "Repent!" A God and a History, a Community . . . but what a haircut!

There is a truth, and there is a falsehood, in this portrait of John. The truth in the image is that John *is* intended to jar the readers of Mark, to shock our sensibilities. His presence sounds a willful note of discord in the initial harmonies of the gospel narrative. John is as out of place as a day-glow orange "Ye Must Be Born Again" sign alongside a tranquil country highway.

But what is genuinely shocking about John is not his weirdness. This is the falsehood in the popular conception of him. He is intended, not to excite the readers' fascination with the bizarre, but to jolt them with a memory. John is not an exotic; he is a living anachronism. His vestments are not outlandish; they are the clothing of the past. John is not "Stranger in Paradise;" he is "Auld Lang Syne." To be precise, John is dressed like the old prophet Elijah, no question about it, and the moment of his appearing is as sobering in its context as would be the arrival of Thomas Jefferson, waving a copy of the Declaration of Independence, in today's Senate chamber.

So, now we know that John is not out of this world, he is simply out of sync . . . but so what? Simply put, if we do not understand that John represents the past, we also cannot understand what he has to say about the future. John, like Jesus who follows him, preaches a message of repentance, but "repentance" is a slippery word, a "weasel word," as someone else has phrased it. We cannot fill it with meaning for our lives until we have come to grips with this character who has stepped out of the pages of the Old Testament and into the pages of the New.

Some people, for instance, think of repentance as something which just naturally happens to people as they move along through the journey of life. We travel along the track, accelerating smoothly, our goals established, our values set, when . . . wham . . . we crash into the wall of some experience we cannot handle, for which our resources are inadequate. *Our* loved one dies, or *we* get rejected by the school of our choice, or *we* have a heart attack, or *we* are laid off from our work. It happens in one form or another to everyone, and such experiences call for a changing of goals, a reformulation of values, an alteration of the ways we cope with life and make our key decisions.

This is, of course, a kind of repentance, but only a mild form. It is really more like growth, or maturation, since, in most such experiences, we do not draw a new hand, but only make a few discards and rearrange the cards we have. We adjust, but do not fundamentally change. This is not the kind of repentance preached by John the Baptizer.

There are others for whom repentance is a larger, more profound, and more theological version of a New Year's resolution. The old year passes to the new, and we feel the extra inches around our waist, or taste the bitter nicotine on our tongue, or think of the hurtful and spiteful things we have said to one near to us, and we repent. We toss the butter pecan ice cream into the disposal, flush the Marlboros down the commode, or stammer out a few long-overdue words of affection and affirmation.

When we repent in this fashion, what we are doing is repudiating our past, wiping the slate clean, turning over a new leaf, beginning all over again. Carl Jung was groping toward this when he wrote,

In the second half of life the necessity is imposed:

• *Of recognizing no longer the validity of our former ideals, but of their contraries;*

• *Of perceiving the error in what previously was our conviction;*

• *Of sensing the untruth in what was our truth . . .*[2]

In his article "Returning to Church," which appeared in the *New York Times Magazine,* novelist Dan Wakefield movingly described his own repentance, a turn from despair to faith. Wakefield portrayed a treacherous time in his life. A long-standing relationship with a woman had just dissolved. He was out of money, and had just buried, within the span of seven months, both of his parents. His work no longer satisfied him, and drugs had become an all too attractive means of escape. "I was," he wrote, "headed for the edge of a cliff." A chance conversation in a neighborhood bar with a housepainter, who was looking for a place to go to mass on Christmas Eve, led to Wakefield's own attendance at a Christmas candle-
light service, then to participation in other services of worship and Bible studies, and to a gradually developing devotional life.

As Wakefield's religious involvement increased, he experienced a growing freedom from his sense of drifting purposelessness and from what he called "my assortment of life-numbing addictions." He wrote:

. . . at some point or other they felt as if they were "lifted," taken away . . . The only concept I know to describe such experience is that of "grace," and the accompanying adjective "amazing" comes to mind along with it.[3]

Christians are familiar with this, the deepest form of a certain kind of repentance, and indeed we celebrate it. "Once I was blind, but now I see,'' we sing. Christians rejoice in the kind of repentance which buries the rags of a soiled past in favor of the white garments of a new future. But even though this comes closer to John's message, this is not yet fully the kind of repentance which John proclaimed.

The repentance John preached is not a mid-course correction; it is more radical than that. The repentance John preached is not a repudiation of the past; it is more complex than that. The repentance John preached calls for a *revising* of the past. It calls for us to look behind before we dare to move ahead. It calls for us to encounter the past we have lived through but have not fully experienced, the past we have inherited but not inhabited, before we enter a future we do not yet comprehend.

What does this mean? Consider the experience of a business executive on the verge of implementing a shrewd business plan. The scheme involved temporarily dropping prices below the level of profitability in order to starve a smaller competitor out of the market. Then, with the market to himself, prices and profits could rise. The fact that the competitor was a struggling family-owned business, not really a major factor in the market, but the sole livelihood of a family with three small children, was known to the executive. The plan was technically legal, though, and all competitors are fair game, since business, after all, is business.

Just as the arrangements were nearly in place, the executive was called back to his hometown for the funeral of a cousin. During the graveside service, as the man sat under the funeral tent which was stretched over the family plot, his eye fell on the gravestone of his grandmother, who had died when he was only a boy. Inscribed on her stone were words from the Book of Proverbs: "She opens her mouth with wisdom, and the teaching of kindness is on her tongue.''

"The teaching of kindness . . .'' The words seemed to be written in fire as they burned in his heart. He had read them many times before on nostalgic visits to the cemetery, but now they leapt from the past into his life. He did not merely recall his grandmother; he was confronted by her memory, judged by the commitments he vaguely knew she held, but had not considered to have any claim on his life. It was a strange and disturbing experience, and he returned to his city with no will to destroy, but to seek somehow to know and live "the teaching of kindness."

The essayist and short story writer Eudora Welty wrote in *One Writer's Beginning* about the deep insight which can result when people explore memories of experiences they thought they already fully understood. "Connections slowly emerge . . . cause and effect begin to align themselves . . . And suddenly a light is thrown back, as when your train rounds a curve, showing there has been a mountain of meaning rising behind you on the way you've come, is rising there still . . ."[4]

A mountain of meaning rising behind you . . . rising there still. *That* is the soil of the repentance John preached. John wears the clothing of an old prophet, *embodies* the history of God's people, in order to proclaim that all that God has done before, which we did not fully see, all that God has said in our memory, which we did not fully believe, has pointed to this moment, to the coming of the Messiah.

What does this repentance look like in our lives?

Whenever we return to an old and well-worn passage in the Bible and do not, through nostalgia or willfulness, force it to say only what we expect it to say, but allow it to encounter us anew, creating new and demanding possibilties for our lives, we have repented.

Whenever we invoke some experience in our memory and discover, in our remembering, more evidence of the hand of God there than we first saw, more signs of the grace of God than we ever knew were there before, more call for gratitude to God than we have yet expressed, and we find in ourselves a will to live a different, more faithful and obedient tomorrow because of what we have discerned, we have repented.

Whenever we return to the faith we have been given, to the gospel we have heard so often, to the stories which have been told again and again, and find there not a retreat, but a renewal. Whenever we discover that all that God has done in our common yesterdays is pointing us anew to the Christ who comes this day, to forgive our sins and to make possible a tomorrow of faith and joy, we have repented.

Notes

[1] Jay McInerney, *Bright Lights, Big City* (New York: Vintage Books, 1984), p. 57.

[2] Carl Jung, as quoted in Bernard Martin, *If God Does Not Die* (Richmond, Virginia: John Knox Press, 1966), p. 9.

[3] Dan Wakefield, "Returning to Church," *The New York Times Magazine* (December 22, 1985), p. 26.

[4] Eudora Welty, *One Writer's Beginnings* (Cambridge, Massachusetts: Harvard University Press, 1984), p. 90.

There's a Man Going Around Taking Names

There is an old black gospel song from the American south, most often sung to the driving beat of a blues guitar, which includes the following lyrics:

There's a man going around taking names.
There's a man going around taking names.
He took my father's name,
And he left my heart in pain.
There's a man going around taking names.

There's a man going around taking names.
There's a man going around taking names.
He took my mother's name,
And he left my heart in pain.
There's a man going around taking names.

There's a man going around taking names.
There's a man going around taking names.
He took my sister's name,
And he left my heart in pain.
There's a man going around taking names.[1]

In the song, the "man going around taking names" is a metaphor, of course, for all that menaces human relationships and life — most prominently, the slave trader and, finally, death itself. And it is a fascinating image for potential evil, this idea of "taking names." Even school children can identify with it. "Now children," warns the teacher. "I'm going to the office for a few minutes, and I'm appointing Frances to be the monitor. Don't misbehave or she will write down your name, and you'll have to deal with me when I get back.' . . . There's somebody around here taking names.

When John the Baptizer was at work in Bethany, beyond the Jordan River, a delegation of religious officials showed up from Jerusalem. They were not there, by the way, on a package tour of the Holy Land; they were there taking names. You could tell that from the very first words to come from their mouths. "Who are you?" they said. No small talk. No pictures of grandchildren passed around. Just, "Who are you?" . . . There are some people going around taking names.

There is a difference, of course, between name-seeking and name-taking. Name-seeking is usually gentle, an innocent desire to know another person. The sales rep you have just met at the convention leans over to squint at your "Hello! I'm _____" badge. The woman who has just moved into the apartment next door meets you at the mail box, extends her hand saying, "I'm Jane Morris in 4-B," and arches an eyebrow expectantly, hoping for your name in return. This is name-seeking.

Name-taking, however, does not want to *know* another person; it wants to put the other person *on trial*. "Let me see your license," says the motorcycle cop, and we respond, "Yes, officer, have I done something wrong?" We sense we are already on trial. "I'm sorry," says the clerk, "I can't take your check without proper I.D." And so we pull out the credit cards and the photo identification as if to say, "See, these will testify in the court of respectability to my good character."

Name-taking places a person on trial, puts a person under threat of judgment, and, naturally makes us wary. Bill collectors roaming through poor, but tightly-knit, neighborhoods often discover that folks somehow cannot recall their neighbors' names, even though they have lived next door to them for thirty years. Or again, I was once the relatively innocent victim of a traffic mishap. A young man, deciding at the last minute to turn into a service station, steered too sharply and creased the fender of my car. Half a dozen people watched the accident happen, but when I approached each of them, seeking an independent witness, they were suddenly struck by a strange combination of blindness and amnesia. They had seen nothing, could not even call up the memory of their own names. Name-taking puts a person on trial, drags them unwillingly into court . . . There's a man going around taking names.

"Who are you?" said the officials from Jerusalem, taking names, and quickly John moved from being a minister at work to being a man under a threat. In fact, John was now on trial. The emissaries from Jerusalem had come as judge, jury, and prosecution to put John's ministry to the test, and John was being called to the stand as the only witness for his own defense. The People of Jerusalem versus John the Baptizer. Will the witness please state his name? Who are you? . . . There's a man around here taking names.

But it is right at this point in the story that something very strange happens. The closest parallel to it I know about occurred in one of Woody Allen's antic movies. The scene in the movie is a courtroom, and a trial is underway. A somber judge is presiding, the jury is listening intently, the prosecuting attorney is laying out the case. Suddenly the rear doors of the courtroom swing open and a frantic, emotionally-distressed man enters. He looks wildly around, and then blurts out a tearful confession, admitting to the astonished court that he, and not the defendant, is the guilty party. A dramatic and startled silence fills the room. The only problem is that the crime to which he has confessed has nothing to do with the case being tried in that court. Slowly a puzzled look gathers on the guilty man's face. Looking anxiously at the judge, he names a particular case and asks if this is the correct court. "Next courtroom," responds the judge, pointing to the exit, and the man bolts out the door.

Just so, as soon as John had been placed under interrogation, he blurted out a confession, but, strangely enough, it was a confession which belonged in another courtroom, was pertinent to another trial: "He confessed, he did not deny, but confessed, 'I am not the Christ.' "(John 1:20) The authorities had come for an affidavit about John; John provides a testimony about the Christ. There are two trials going on here. The officials are conducting one, but John insists upon being a witness in the other. They attempt to put John to the test, but, ironically, his testimony turns the tables and places them on trial. Indeed, if we listen to the court record, we can hear the overlap of the two proceedings, feel the mounting frustration of the prosecutors as their key witness gives his deposition in a case they did not even know was being tried:

Prosecution: What, then, are you Elijah?

John: I am not.

Prosecution: Are you the prophet?

John: No.

Prosecution: Who are you, then? Tell us about *yourself.* Answer the court.

John: I can speak about myself only by speaking of someone else. I cry in the wilderness, announcing the coming of another.

[The prosecution asks for a brief recess to confer. The interrogation then resumes.]

Prosecution: This is confusing. Why, then, are you baptizing?

John: I baptize with water, but there is one standing in this court at this very moment, and you do not do know him. I am not worthy to untie his sandals.

Back and forth it went, the questions and the answers, the authorities conducting one trial, John giving his witness in another, until finally we are left to wonder which trial is real. Is John the defendant, or the officials? Is it John on trial, or is it the world?

The earliest Christians must have heard this story of John's interrogation with great enthusiasm, and perhaps even a measure of joyous laughter. They heard it as a story about the day they put old John the Baptizer on trial, and he stood up and gave his witness to Jesus in a greater courtroom, one in which his accusers had no power. They also remembered the day they tried to take Jesus' name, the day they brought Jesus himself into court, and how he, too, turned the tables and put the accuser on the stand:

> *"Are you the King of the Jews?" said Pilate.*

> *"Do you say this . . . ?" responded Jesus, turning his accuser into the defendant.*

> "Me? *Am I a Jew? . . . What have* you *done?"*

> *"I bear witness to the truth. Everyone who is of the truth hears my voice."*

> *"What is truth?" asked Pilate, convicting himself.*

In his provocative book *Liturgies and Trials,* Richard K. Fenn has commented that "the question of whether it is God or Caesar who is on trial is at the heart of the biblical tradition . . ."[2] Christians are persuaded that it is the world which is finally on trial, and they give their testimony accordingly. Placing their trust in the Christ who "will come to judge the quick and the dead," the Christian community has been bold to face all worldly accusers, whether they come from Rome with swords, from Birmingham with police dogs, from Warsaw with a rifle, from Hollywood with a sneer, or from

Washington with a court order. As the folk hymn puts it, "All my trials, Lord, soon be over."

Fenn has also observed that contemporary life is a constant experience of being placed in the box and put on trial. Students in school must produce their papers, grades, and SAT scores "for the record." In a career, one is always having to demonstrate competence and justify actions. A stockholders' meeting places the achievements of the corporate officers on trial. Single people and divorced people are often accused in the court of gossip of being unable to maintain long-term relationships. Parents enroll in "effectiveness training" seminars, lest they be found guilty of inadequate methods of raising their children. And now that dozens of paperback books have mapped the dark regions of the unconscious, there is opened up, according to Fenn, "a source of accusations or of offensive motives that turns a lifetime into a perpetual trial with fresh evidence continually arising from buried sources."[3] . . . There's always somebody going around taking names.

We are under constant trial, and it is no wonder, then, that one of the ways Christians have always understood the good news of what has happened in Jesus Christ is in terms of already being acquitted in the highest court of all. The Apostle Paul once asked, "Who shall bring any charge against God's elect? . . . Who is to condemn?" The answer: No one, because the Judge himself was the very one who died for us, was raised from the dead, and even now prays for us. (Romans 8:34)

The world places us on trial every day, but what the world does not know is that we have already been tried in a greater court and, through the mercy of Christ, we have been found "not guilty." Like John, the Christian community knows that there are two trials going on. The accusations and condemnations of the world are painful, but they finally have no lasting power, because our case has been pled before another judge in whom there is no condemnation. "There stands among you," said John to his accusers, "one whom you do not know," and when, the next day, John saw Jesus himself, he continued his testimony in the trial which really matters, "Behold the Lamb of God, who takes away the sin of the world!" The accusers of the world try to take our names, but in Jesus Christ we have been given a new name, and the world cannot ever take it.

> There stands a tree in paradise,
> and the pilgrims call it "The Tree of Life;"
> All my trials, Lord, soon be over.

In the television series *Roots* there is a scene in which the slave traders are trying to break the spirit of the young black man named Kunta Kinte, whom they have captured and brought to America from his African homeland. They have tied him to a tree, and with whips they are attempting to beat into him a new and submissive identity. "Your name is Toby," they say. The young man resists, and the whips fall. "Your name is Toby." More resistance, and the whips fall again and again. Finally the punishment is too severe, and the young man hangs his head in defeat and speaks his slave name, "Toby."

I once heard a black minister speak of his own enraged reaction when he saw that episode. He admitted that, for a moment, he was consumed with hatred, not only for those who were beating Kunta Kinte, but for all white people, for all who, through the whip of racism, bring humiliation and shame to others. The only thing that kept this hatred from settling into his heart, he said, was the deep awareness of his faith in another man, a man who was also tied to a tree and beaten. "They took this man's life," he said, "but they never took his name. And one day every knee will bow and every tongue will confess that name. Jesus is Lord."

Notes

1. "There's a Man Going Around Taking Names," from *Religious Music: Solo and Performance* (Album number 15 in The Library of Congress "Folk Music in America" series, 1978) Words in the public domain.

2. Richard K. Fenn, *Liturgies and Trials: The Secularization of Religious Language* (New York: The Pilgrim Press, 1982), p. 49.

3. *Ibid.*, p. 27.

Where's the Treasure?

When I was a child there was a game we would play in our neighborhood to pass the time on rainy afternoons. It was a game of the imagination, and if it had a name, which I don't think it did, it would have been called "Where Would You Leave the Treasure?" The idea was this: Suppose you had a large amount of money, a treasure really, but some unexpected-crisis has come up, and suddenly you have to leave the treasure with someone for safekeeping. You can't put it in the bank or bury it under the oak tree in the back yard — there isn't time. The rule of the game is that you have to *entrust* it to someone, some human being. Whom would you choose? The fun of the game, of course, was sitting around in a circle and exploring all the character flaws and virtues of the various possibilities, searching for a trustworthy person.

"How about the school principal?" someone would suggest.

'Nah, he'd probably steal it."

"Well, how about the preacher?"

"Too risky. He'd probably put it in the collection plate."

"OK, then, what about your sister?"

"Are you kidding? She'd want to split it"

And on it would go, the search for just the right person to keep the treasure. In the mind of a child, the stakes were high: your whole treasure risked on something as fragile as the trustworthiness of another human being.

Now, one way to read the first chapter of the Gospel of Luke is as a divine version of "Where Would You Leave the Treasure?" God was searching for some place in human life to leave the treasure. In God's case, the treasure was not gold, but the gospel. The treasure was not silver, but news . . . good news. Not cold, hard cash, but the deep, rich, and abiding promise that, when all is said and done, we are not alone, that God is finally "God with us," at work in our world, setting things right. That's the treasure. Despite appearances to the contrary, there is coming a time when swords will be beaten into plowshares, and peace will flow like a river. That's the treasure. The day is coming when justice will cover the earth like the sea, and empty barns, and empty stomachs, and empty hearts will be filled with grain and honey, joy and hope, and the dark stain of human destruction will be bleached clean by the grace of God. That's the treasure.

Now, where in the world do you leave a treasure like that? More fragile than silver, in a way, and yet infinitely more valuable. A treasure able to be squandered, dismissed, rationalized, even crucified. Where do you leave a treasure like that so that it will be preserved, cherished, and allowed to grow?

That's what Luke wants to tell us. Luke wants to tell us the story of where God decided to leave the treasure, and this is the way he begins: "In the days of Herod, king of Judea . . . " (Luke 1:5), almost as if to say, "Now there's a possibility!" God could have left the treasure with the Herods of the world, with the politicians, the ones who pave the roads and collect the taxes, the ones who build the schools and pass the laws, the ones who command the armies and provide for the care of the weak. God could have left the treasure with the Herods, and it's not as strange a possibility as it might at first seem, because, after all, the treasure is in part *political*. The treasure is the news that God is at work in the world to pull tyrants off their high horses and to lift up those who hunger and thirst for justice. That when one more starving child in Africa — or anywhere else — dies, something at the heart of

God dies, too. That God is at work to break the deadlocks, to fill the bowls with food, and to send the greedy away empty. That every valley shall be exalted and every mountain and hill made low — and that's not real estate; that's politics!

And since it is politics, it would have made a certain kind of sense for God to have entrusted the treasure to the movers and the shakers — the Herods of the world.

But God did not leave the treasure with Herod, because the gospel is the good news that, if there is to be justice in the world, there can only be one true King. If there is peace in the world, there can only be one true Ruler. If there is to be mercy, there can only be one true Lord . . . and his name is not Herod.

Every year at the Metropolitan Museum of Art in New York, there is displayed, beneath the great Christmas tree, a beautiful eighteenth century Neapolitan nativity scene. In many ways it is a very familiar scene. The usual characters are all there: shepherds roused from sleep by the voices of angels; the exotic wisemen from the East seeking, as Auden once put it, "how to be human now"; Joseph; Mary; the babe — all are there, each figure an artistic marvel of wood, clay, and paint. There is, however, something surprising about this scene, something unexpected here, easily missed by the casual observer. What is strange here is that the stable, and the shepherds, and the cradle are set, not in the expected small town of Bethlehem, but among the ruins of mighty Roman columns. The fragile manger is surrounded by broken and decaying columns. The artists knew the meaning of the treasure: The gospel, the birth of God's new age, was also the death of the old world.[1]

Herods know in their souls what we perhaps have passed over too lightly: God's presence in the world means finally the end of their own power. They seek not to preserve the treasure, but to crush it. For Herod, the gospel is news too bad to be endured, and Luke wants us to see that God had to find another place to leave the treasure.

"In the days of Herod . . . there was a priest named Zechariah . . ." (Luke 1:5), Luke tells us, and there's another possibility. God could have left the treasure with the Zechariahs of the world, the ones who think holy thoughts, handle holy things, and perform holy deeds. God could have left the treasure with the Zechariahs, and it's not a strange thought, because Zechariah is a priest. Priests are theologians of a sort, and, after all, the treasure is, in part, *theological*. The treasure is the good news that it is *God* who is at work to set things right, that it is *God* who gathers up all efforts of human good will and gives them strength beyond their measure, mercy beyond their depth, and hope beyond their grandest dreams. It is *God* who has made us, and *God* who is with us, and *God* who reclaims us, and not we ourselves. So, Zechariah, a man who handles holy things, and thinks holy thoughts, and performs holy deeds, would be a good place to leave the treasure.

There are signs that God did indeed consider leaving the treasure with his priest Zechariah. Zechariah was an ordinary priest, with the ordinary priestly responsibilities of burning incense and making sacrifices up at the Temple, and he had done the ordinary thing of marrying Elizabeth, herself the daughter of a priest. But he and Elizabeth had one very extraordinary problem. They had no children — could have no children — for Elizabeth was barren, and for reasons which have to do with the culture of the first century, that was a pain to them both and an embarrassment to Elizabeth. Then, one day in the Temple, when Zechariah was lighting the incense, God — almost as a way of testing to see if Zechariah were a good place to leave the treasure — gave Zechariah a taste of the good news, an anticipatory touch of the treasure. An angel appeared to Zechariah and told him, "Do not be afraid, your prayer has been answered. You will have great joy and gladness. Your wife will become pregnant and bear a son."

It was then that Zechariah, who thought holy thoughts, and handled holy things, and performed holy deeds, showed that he was not the place to leave the treasure. Zechariah, so familiar with the holy, finally could not believe the presence of the holy when it intruded into his life. "How shall I know this?" he whined. "I need proof. I'm an old man. This is impossible. My wife is an old woman. How shall I know this? I need proof."

And in a scene of great sadness, the angel reaches forth toward Zechariah's lips, saying, "You will be silent. You will be unable to speak, for you did not believe my words." There is a familiarity with the holy which, ironically, produces a numbness to the holy, and Zechariah was not the place to leave the treasure. For Herod, the gospel was news too bad to be endured. For Zechariah, it was too amazing to be believed, too good to be true.

There is a well-known legend about a seminary student approaching the great theologian Paul Tillich. Tillich had just lectured on the authority of the Scripture, and the student was clutching in his hand a large, black, leather-bound Bible. "Do you believe this is the Word of God?" shouted the student.

Tillich looked at the student's fingers tightly gripping the book. "Not if you think you can grasp it," said Tillich. "Only when the Bible grasps you." There is an over-familiarily with things holy, which, ironically, can make us numb to the intrusion of the holy in our lives.

The novelist and essayist Annie Dillard has written about this kind of over-familiarity with the holy. She says that she does not find Christians, outside of those who worshiped in the catacombs, "sufficiently sensible of conditions." She thinks of church people in worship as children who think they are playing around with a chemistry set, but who are actually mixing up a batch of TNT. She maintains

> It is madness to wear ladies' straw hats and velvet hats to worship; we should all be wearing crash helmets. Ushers should issue life preservers and signal flares; they should lash us to our pews.[2]

God did not leave the treasure with the Herods; they would

crush it. God did not leave the treasure with the Zechariahs: they could not believe it. God did not leave the treasure in the courthouse or in the sanctuary. God did not leave the treasure in the palace or under the altar. It is now that Luke tells us the surprise: God left the treasure in a place which was in that time the weakest of all places, the least likely of all spots — the womb of a woman. And Luke also tells us that the first time that the gospel is proclaimed by human lips, it is not in the Roman Senate or in the Holy of Holies; it is not by Caesar, or Peter, or Paul. It is in a place the world would count for nothing: a conversation between two women, Mary and Elizabeth, facing their pregnancies. God left the treasure in a woman's womb, and it is in a conversation about stretch marks and swollen ankles that the treasure is first proclaimed.

For Herod, the news was too bad to be endured. For Zechariah it was news too amazing to be believed. But for Mary, too unimportant to be counted, it was, in Frederick Buechner's phrase, "too good not to be true."

Maybe Luke wants us to know that the treasure of the gospel, which will one day fill the earth with its power, must first be planted in those weak and helpless places which yearn for it the most, hunger for it most deeply, and thus can believe and cherish it most fully.

There is a scene in Tennessee Williams' *A Streetcar Named Desire* when Blanche, an unlovely person desperately seeking love, meets Mitch, a man who is grossly overweight, who is embarrassed that he perspires profusely, and who, like Blanche, is frantically lonely. It is not their strength, but their mutual weakness, which brings them together, and because they are both so needy, Blanche is able to trust Mitch with the tragic story of her life. Mitch then takes her in his arms and says, "You need somebody, and I need somebody, too. Could it be you and me, Blanche?"

She looks at him in amazement, then reaches for him, her eyes filling with tears, and says, "Sometimes there's God, so quickly."[3]

It is the places of weakness in our lives and in the world which are most open to the amazing intrusion of God's presence. And part of the good news is that it is precisely there where God leaves the treasure. God does not come to that part of us which swaggers through life, confident in our self-sufficiency. God, rather, leaves the treasure in the broken places where we know we cannot make it on our own. God does not come to us in that part of us which brushes aside all who threaten our status, all who bore or bother us. God comes to us in those rare moments when we transcend our own selfishness long enough to glimpse the needs of others and to feel those needs deeply enough to hunger and thirst for God to set it right. As the old hymn puts it:

When other helpers fail,
and comforts flee,
Help of the helpless,
O abide with me.[4]

On the wall of the museum of the concentration camp at Dachau is a moving photograph of a mother and her little girl being taken to the gas chamber at Auschwitz. The girl, who is walking in front of her mother, does not know where she is going. The mother, who walks behind, does know, but there is nothing, absolutely nothing, the mother can do to stop this tragedy. In her helplessness, she performs the only act of love left to her. She places her hand over her little girl's eyes so, at least, she will not have to see the horror which faces her. When people see this picture in the museum, they do not move quickly or easily to the next one. You can feel their emotion, almost hear their cries, "O God, don't let that be all there is. Somewhere, somehow, set things right."

Luke's word to us this day is that God hears those prayers, and that it is into just such situations of hopelessness and helplessness that the power of God is born. It is there that God entrusts the treasure, lifting up the lowly and filling the hungry with good things — setting things right.

On a dark night in a feed stall in Bethlehem, the treasure which was entrusted to Mary became the treasure for us all. All the Herods and all the priests and all the powers-that-be gathered around to do their worst. But on Easter morning, just as Mary said, "God stretched out his mighty arm . . ."

Notes

[1] From Thomas G. Long, "Foreword," *Journal for Preachers,* Vol. I, No. 1 (Advent, 1981), p. 3.

[2] Annie Dillard, *Teaching a Stone to Talk* (New York: Harper and Row Publishers, 1982), p. 40.

[3] Tennessee Williams, "A Streetcar Named Desire," as quoted in Sharon Blessum Sawatzky, "Sometimes There's God So Quickly," *Spinning a Sacred Yarn* (New York: Pilgrim Press, 1981), p. 188.

[4] Henry F. Lyte, "Abide With Me: Fast Falls the Eventide." Words in the public domain.

Shepherds and Bathrobes

Sometimes the events described in the Bible bowl us over with their sheer size. The picture in Genesis of God commanding light and darkness to go their separate ways, summoning the seven seas like chargers, and, with a word, drawing up the massive continents from the primordial ooze of the formless earth. That's scale! Or, hundreds of thundering Egyptian chariots dashing headlong after the fleeing Hebrew slaves. Suddenly the once dry gap in the sea is invaded by a violent wall of water, foam filling the nostrils of horses, their eyes white with fear. Horsemen are thrown from their mounts. Charioteers are swept away by the swirling torrent. Then a death-marked stillness settles on the surface of the sea. Immense! Or again, the vision in the Book of Revelation of the saints in heaven gathered in a multitude greater than the eye can see, an ocean of faces and white robes larger than the mind can measure, an endless throng finding the place in their hymn-books, and triumphantly singing, "Hallelujah! Salvation and glory and power belong to our God!" Compared to this the Mormon Tabernacle Choir sounds like a quartet.

In the face of scenes of such magnitude, the church's attempts to make them come alive in worship has seemed like a frail and tiny vessel, a thimble dipped into the ocean. How do mere sermons and hymns, prayers and readings, anthems and responses encompass events of such breadth and height?

William Sloane Coffin, the pastor of New York City's Riverside Church, once told of the Easter sunrise service held annually on the rim of the Grand Canyon. As the resurrection account was read about the angel rolling away the stone from the tomb, a massive boulder was pushed over the edge and the congregation watched it crash mightily into the depths of the canyon. "Too dramatic?" asks Coffin. "No," he replies, "the Gospel message itself demands such drama."[2]

Tonight is Christmas Eve, and the familiar story we have heard from Luke's Gospel is itself one of those events which threatens to overwhelm us by its scope. It begins, to be sure in a small and gentle way, shepherds resting on a Judean hillside keeping wary watch over the flocks. But suddenly the episode spills beyond the edges of imagination's canvas. The night sky is flooded by the light of glory. First there is one angel, then another and another, until finally there is a heavenly host, putting on an angelic display so terrifyingly spectacular that the King James Bible seems deeply understated when it reports that the shepherds "were sore afraid."

Tonight, all across the land, in fellowship halls, sanctuaries, and church basements, those who know and love this story will try to re-create it, and the results, compared to the original, will seem pitiably small. A gaggle of neighborhood boys, the very ones we have seen kicking a soccer ball across the front yard, will stand on a hillside of indoor-outdoor carpet, guarding cardboard and cotton-ball sheep with makeshift staffs, their terry-cloth bathrobes almost, but not quite, hiding their worn Adidas sneakers. Suddenly a gauzily angelic version of the little girl from next door will burst onto the scene, lisping the good news through the gap where her next tooth will eventually grow. Other angels will soon join her, their foil-wrapped wings bouncing wildly to the beat of "Gloria in Excelsis." When the angels have fluttered to stage right, the shepherds will lumber left to Bethlehem to find a fawn-eyed Mary and a sheepish Joseph, whose steady downward gaze is fixed upon the blanket-wrapped doll in the plywood creche.

These bathrobe Christmas pageants, and indeed *all* of our attempts to convey the range and power of whatever-in-the-name-of-God happened that night to those shepherds, seem so weak and small. They appear to dim the blinding luminosity of those moments to the flicker of a single candle, to reduce the size of those great events to the scale of a Hallmark Christmas card. As the essayist Annie Dillard once put it,

> . . . *if you send any shepherds a Christmas card on which is printed a three-by-three photograph of the angel of the Lord, the glory of the Lord, and a multitude of the heavenly host, they will not be sore afraid.*[3]

Perhaps this is so, but before we put the bathrobes back into the closet and dismantle the plywood crib, we should look again and carefully at the way in which Luke describes this event. The important thing to notice is that Luke does not dazzle us with spacious description. How bright was this shining glory of the Lord? Luke does not say. What did the angels look like? Luke is silent. How many were there? Luke declines to count them. What exactly were the angels doing as they filled the sky with song? Luke has no comment. What expression was on the face of the newborn savior? Luke says nothing. It is as if Luke pulls our attention away from the events themselves and focuses it instead on something else, namely the *responses* of those who were involved. The shepherds were "sore afraid," but returned from Bethlehem "glorifying and praising God for all they had heard and seen." The people who heard their reports "wondered at what the shepherds had told them." Mary "kept all these things, pondering them in her heart." As for the "glory of the Lord," Luke is reticent, but when it comes to those upon whom it shone, he breaks his descriptive silence and saves his fullest language to portray what happened in their lives and hearts.

Frederick Buechner tells in one of his sermons about some useful advice he once received from a young ship's officer aboard a British freighter. It was night; the ship was in the middle of the Atlantic Ocean, and the officer had been peering into the darkness, looking for the lights of other ships. He told Buechner that the way to see lights on the horizon is not to look straight at the horizon, but to look just above the horizon. You can see the lights better, he told Buechner, when you do not try to look at them *directly.* "Since then," writes Buechner, "I have learned that it is also the way to see other things."[4]

Just so, Luke moves our gaze from the light on the horizon to the places just above, below, and off to one side. We are told of the light which filled the world that night, but we do not really *see* it. We see instead the reflection of that light on the faces and in the hearts of those who were present.

Surely one of the reasons Luke does this is because he knew how arrogant it would be to attempt to do otherwise. What pushed back the darkness that night was nothing less than the glory of God, and human language and action simply cannot scale those heights. To try to do so risks vanity at best, idolatry at worst. I once attended the annual Christmas show at New York's Radio City Music Hall, and an impressive show it was. After entertaining presentations of seasonal chestnuts, like Dicken's "A Christmas Carol," the review moved to its finale, a recreation of the nativity itself. In command of a stage the size of a city block and with the virtually unlimited resources of Broadway at their disposal, the producers were not at all reluctant to attempt to give us a taste of the real thing. There were no neighborhood kids wandering uneasily around the sets here. These shepherds were professional actors in authentic garb. Real sheep and camels made their way to center stage, where a matinee-idol Joseph and a Mary of breath-taking beauty cuddled a live, irresistibly precious, baby Jesus. Above the scene was a flashing, electric star, several stories high, surrounded by fluttering angels projected almost magically from a booth in the rear. Handel's "Hallelujah Chorus" filled the theater with several hundred decibels of bone-vibrating sound. The place jumped with light and movement, and the audience scarcely knew where to look. It was a massive spectacle, which lacked only one thing — the glory of the Lord. The very attempt to look directly at this moment, to replicate its majestic size, had, ironically, drained it of all mystery. Everyone's eyes were filled, but no one pondered anything in her heart.

But there is another, and more important, reason why Luke turns our gaze from the light itself toward the faces of those people who were illumined by it. Luke wants us to search those faces and to find our *own* faces reflected there, to find *ourselves* once again filled with wonder, to ponder these things in *our* hearts, to contemplate the possibility that *we,* too, might glorify and praise God this Christmas Eve for all that we have experienced because of the life of the Christ child born that night. As New Testament scholar Raymond Brown stated it, the shepherds "are the forerunners . . . of future believers who will glorify God for what they have heard and will praise God for what they have seen."[5] Luke does not want us to be fascinated by this story's height; he invites us instead to explore for ourselves its depth.

There was once a Christmas pageant at a small church in which the part of the innkeeper at Bethlehem was played by a high school student. He was a quiet and polite boy, but the kind of boy for whom the word "awkward" was an apt description — awkward in manner, awkward in social relationships, even awkward in size, his growing frame always pushing at the limits of his clothing. His peers liked him well enough, but he was the sort of person who was easy to overlook, to exclude from the center of things. When Joseph and Mary appeared at the inn, he stood . . . awkwardly . . . in the doorway, slumping a bit toward the couple as they made their request for lodging. He then dutifully recited his one line, "There is no room in the inn." But as Mary and Joseph turned and walked wearily away toward the cattle stall where they would spend the night, the boy continued to watch them with eyes filled with compassion. Suddenly responding to a grace which, though not part of the script, filled the moment, he startled himself, the holy couple, and the audience, by calling, "Wait a minute. Don't go. You can have my room."

And that is why, when all is said and done, those Christmas pageants in church fellowship halls, sanctuaries, and basements perhaps capture the Christmas story best. They are, like Luke's gospel itself, pictures of what happens to unremarkable people in a dark world when suddenly, and in ways they do not fully understand, the glory of the Lord shines upon them. Like the characters in Luke, the players in these pageants do not pretend to express the light; they only try to reflect it. The cast, drawn from those who populate our workaday lives, embodies in its very ordinariness the truth of the angel's promise, "Unto *you* is born this day a Savior." There is the kid from down the street, wearing a tinfoil crown and carrying a cigar box of frankincense. There is our daughter, adjusting her wire halo as she lauds, "My soul magnifies the Lord." And there we are, too, staffs in hand, stumbling over each other to get near the newborn King, our unsteady voices searching for the correct pitch as we sing anew, "O come let us adore Him, O come let us adore Him, Christ the Lord."

Notes

1 Portions of this sermon previously appeared in Thomas G. Long, "Bit Parts in the Christmas Pageant," *Journal for Preachers,* Vol. VI, No. 1 (Advent, 1982), pp. 14-21. This material is used by permission.

2 William Sloane Coffin, "Our Resurrection, Too," in Paul H. Sherry (ed.), *The Riverside Preachers* (New York: The Pilgrim Press, 1978), p. 162.

3 Annie Dillard, *Teaching a Stone to Talk* (New York: Harper and Row, 1982), p. 95.

4 Frederick Buechner, "The End is Life," in *The Magnificent Defeat* (New York: The Seabury Press, 1966), pp. 79-80.

5 Raymond E. Brown, *The Birth of the Messiah* (Garden City, N.Y.: Image Books, 1977), p. 429.

They Also Serve Who Wait

"The whole thing is rotten," said Morris Weiser, as he tapped his cane on the vaulted ceiling of the old and decaying synagogue in New York's lower east side. Morris Weiser was among the few Jews who survived the Janowska concentration camp in Poland, and now, a retired butcher in his seventies, his one remaining passion is to keep alive the Chasam Sopher synagogue. The synagogue has few Sabbath worshipers now, but Morris has put all of his savings into this place, sustains it by his constant effort, keeps it barely alive by the sheer force of his will. "When God saved me from Hitler," he said, "I promised that in any country I come I will do something for God."

The synagogue, like the tenements which fill the neighborhood in which it stands, is marked by peeling paint, deteriorating floors, and falling plaster. Morris, himself, is feeling the wearing effects of the passing days. "I'm broken down like this shul," he confesses.

In the days before the war, Morris had been a promising young medical student, but now his youth is gone, his money is gone, and all he has left are the synagogue and hope. And so, Morris Weiser does what he can, and he waits. Casting his eyes over the vacant pews, he vows that someday "there'll be a lot of Jews here."[1]

Simeon and Anna were also aging Jews who clung to their

hope . . . and waited. Luke tells us that Simeon and Anna lived in Jerusalem and were among those who looked expectantly for God to come in power to save his people. Like Morris, who believes that a God who can save will not leave the synagogue forever empty, Simeon and Anna believed that a God who can save would not leave the chosen people forever empty. And so, like Morris, they did what they could, and they waited. New Testament scholar Raymond Brown gives us the best translation of Luke's descriptions of them: Simeon "was upright and devout, waiting for the consolation of Israel." Anna "never left the Temple courts; day and night she worshiped God, fasting and praying," for she was among "those waiting for the redemption of Israel."[2]

It is never easy to wait for anything of importance — for Christmas, for the plane carrying the one we love, for the morning to relieve the sleepless night, for the healing word in a bitter argument, for the toilsome task to be done, for the labor to be over and the child to be born, for death. It is never easy to wait.

It is hardest of all to wait for God. Not many can bear its harsh discipline. Not many can attain its delicate balance of action and hope. Not many can achieve its deep wisdom. Not many can endure its long and dark hours. Therefore, since the demands of waiting for God are so great, there is always the temptation to transform waiting for God into something else, something less.

There are some who would change waiting for God into passivity. "It is *God* for whom we wait," they say, "so nothing can be done until God comes. Nation will rage against nation, and there is nothing we can do about it. We must wait for God to bring us peace. The poor we will always have with us, and it is God who will take care of them. We live in an evil and unjust world, sad, but true, and we must wait for God to set things right."

But waiting for God is not like sitting in a darkened theater, idly waiting for the movie to begin. Waiting for God is more like waiting for an honored guest to arrive at our home. There is much work to be done; everything must be made ready. Every sweep of the broom, every pressing of the dough, every setting of the table is done in anticipation of the needs and wishes of the one who is to come.

When James Watt was Secretary of the Interior, he often infuriated environmentalists by his careless treatment of the nation's natural resources. He advocated the granting of oil leases in wilderness areas, and he worked to permit strip-mining in areas adjacent to national parks. Particularly troubling was the fact that Watt based his decisions on religious as well as political grounds. A fundamentalist Christian, Watt saw no real reason to preserve the environment, since Jesus would be coming soon. While Watt can perhaps be admired for his unswerving faith in the coming Christ, his actions demonstrated a serious misunderstanding of the Christ who is coming. The Christ for whom we wait is the very one "in whom all things were created," and a selfish lack of care for the creation is no way to wait for his coming.

In the early 1960's, at the height of the civil rights movement, a group of white ministers issued a public statement urging Dr. Martin Luther King, in the name of the Christian faith, to be more patient in his quest for justice and to relax the relentless struggle for civil rights. King's response came in the form of the famous "Letter from Birmingham Jail." In the letter, King indicated that he had received similar requests for delay, indeed, that he had just gotten a letter from a "white brother in Texas" who wrote, ". . . It is possible you are in too great a religious hurry . . . The teachings of Christ take time to come to earth." Dr. King replied that such an attitude stemmed from a sad misunderstanding of time, the notion that time itself cures all ills. Time, King argued, could be used for good or for evil. Human progress, he said, is not inevitable, but rather. . .

> . . . it comes through the tireless efforts of men willing to be co-workers with God, and without this hard work, time itself becomes an ally of the forces of social stagnation. We must use time creatively, in the knowledge that the time is always ripe to do right.[3]

King knew that complete justice must await the coming of God. That was the theme of his final sermon in which he proclaimed, "I've been to the mountaintop. I've seen the promised land." But he was persuaded that while we wait, "the time is always ripe to do right." Simeon and Anna were waiting for God to come, but they also were not passive in their waiting. Simeon was full of devotion and did what was just. Anna kept the lights burning at the Temple with her ceaseless worship. They waited, but, while they waited, they did what they could.

On the other hand, there are others who are weary of waiting for God, who would turn instead to more immediate and tangible sources for action and hope. According to the account in the *New York Times,* it was just before Christmas several years ago that David Storch, a music teacher, borrowed a copy of the score of Handel's "Messiah" from the Brooklyn Public Library. Through a clerical error, however, the transaction was not recorded. There were several other requests for the score, and the library staff, unaware that it had been checked out, spent many hours searching in vain for it through the stacks. On the day that Storch returned it, placing it on the circulation desk, he was astonished to hear the librarian spontaneously, joyously, and loudly shout, "The 'Messiah' is here! The 'Messiah' is back!" Every head in the library turned toward the voice, but, alas, as the *Times* reported, "A few minutes later everyone went back to work."[4]

A wry story, but also a parable of the often dashed expectations of those who wait for God. Someone cries, "Peace, peace," but there is no peace. Another says, "Comfort, comfort," but there is little comfort. "Come, thou long-expected Jesus," goes the prayerful hymn, and heads turn in a moment of curious interest, then, seeing nothing, go back to work. And so, weary of waiting on a God who does not come, we lower our horizons, fold our hands in prayer to more tangible gods to give us purpose, and turn to more immediate and reliable resources for hope. We build shiny sanctuaries of glass and steel where we can celebrate "possibility thinking" and the other human potentials, which we hope will save us from our self-doubt, if not our sins. We fill the silos and the skies with ever more potent weapons of destruction, which we hope will save us from each other. And we summon the elixirs of modern medicine to save us from disease, aging, and finally from death. In short, tired of waiting for the true God, we create our own.

In Arnold Schoenberg's opera "Moses and Aaron," while Moses is on the mountaintop receiving the Law, Aaron is left in the valley to wait with the people. Exhausted, impatient, and deprived of the vision of God's presence, the people cry to Aaron, "Point God out! We want to kneel down . . . But then, where is he? Point him out!" Finally Aaron yields to their plea, forging for them a god they can touch, a god for whom they never have to wait. "O Israel," he says,

> *. . . I return your gods to you,*
> *and also give you to them,*
> *just as you have demanded.*
> *You shall provide the stuff;*
> *I shall give it a form . . .*[4]

But our gods made of positive thoughts, nuclear megatons, management objectives, secular therapies, and cosmetic skill cannot save us. Indeed they become burdens to us, heavy to carry, costly to maintain. It is God alone who saves, and part of what it means to be fully human is to wait for his coming. Jesuit priest William F. Lynch has observed that there are two kinds of waiting. One kind waits because "there is nothing else to do." The other is born out of hope. The decision to engage in this hopeful kind of waiting . . .

> *. . . is one of the great human acts. It includes, surely, the*
> *acceptance of darkness, sometimes its defiance. It includes*
> *the enlarging of one's perspective beyond a present moment*
> *. . . It simply chooses to wait, and in so doing gives the fu-*
> *ture the only chance it has to emerge.*[5]

Simeon and Anna did not wait because "there was nothing else to do," but because they had hope. Therefore their
waiting was not a vacuum, devoid of activity. They worked
and worshiped, performed acts of justice and prayer. While
they waited, they defied the darkness by serving God, because
it was for the light of *God* that they waited. They did what
they could, and they waited.

And, Luke tells us, God did come to them. Who knows
what they were expecting, but surely it was not this: a fragile
baby bundled into the Temple by two young parents who were
eager to obey the ritual law of purification, but who were too
poor to afford the sacrifice of a lamb and brought with them
instead the acceptable substitute, a pair of birds. A man, a
woman, two birds, and a baby. Can this be the heralded and
hoped-for coming of God?

It is hard to wait for God. There are some who wait for
God passively, and there are some who impatiently refuse to
wait, but the hardest part of waiting for God is to recognize
and accept God when he comes and how he comes. We pray
for God to come and give us young people to fill the pews,
and God comes, not bringing more people but a new and
demanding mission. We pray for God to give us inner peace,
and God comes to us bringing another struggle. We pray for
God to come and heal, and God comes to us at graveside saying, "I am the Resurrection and the Life." We pray for God
to come and console his people, and in the front door of the
Temple walk two new and uncertain parents carrying a pair
of birds . . . and a baby who will die on a cross.

But old Anna looked, and somehow she knew that she had
seen the fulfillment of her hope and Israel's hope. Old Simeon
looked, and he knew, too. He knew that God indeed had come,
and he also knew that this coming of God, like all of God's
comings, both met human need and defied human expectation, that it would bring both salvation and demand, great hope
and great cost. As soon as he had said, "Mine eyes have seen
thy salvation," he added the warning, "This child is set for

the fall and rising of many in Israel." Every coming of God meets our needs, but also violates our expectations and demands our lives.

When the master artist Giotto expressed this story in paint, he, too, saw the fulfillment and the demand, the joy and the hope, in the coming of God. His "Presentation in the Temple" is, according to art critic John W. Dixon, Jr., "one of the few genuinely witty paintings in great art."[6] Simeon holds the baby Jesus, his lips moving now beneath his hoary beard, carefully reciting his oft-rehearsed lines, *"Nunc dimittis . . . Now lettest thou thy servant depart in peace."* Giotto knows his Simeon. He also knows his babies, for the infant Jesus, far from resting contentedly through this aria, is responding as all babies do when held by eccentric strangers. His dark eyes are narrowed and fixed in frozen alarm on Simeon. He reaches desperately for his mother, every muscle arched away from the strange old man. Giotto knows his babies. He also knows the deep truth of this moment, for as Jesus reaches away from Simeon toward Mary, we observe that the child is suspended above the temple altar.[7] "This very human baby," observes Dixon, "is from the beginning, the eternal sacrifice for the redemption of mankind."[8]

Redemption and sacrifice. Hope and demand. So it is with the coming of God. But God will come. The God who came to Simeon and Anna will come to us, too, violating our expectations even as he comes to meet our deepest needs. Until He comes, like Anna and Simeon, we do what we can . . . and wait.

Notes

1 Joseph Berger, "A Man Battles to Save Cherished Synagogue," *The New York Times* (July 21, 1986), section B, p. 3.

2 Raymond E. Brown, *The Birth of the Messiah* (Garden City, New York: Doubleday and Company, 1977), pp. 435-6.

[3] Martin Luther King, Jr., "Letter from Birmingham Jail," in *Why We Can't Wait* (New York: Harper and Row, 1964), p. 89.

[4] Arnold Schoenberg, "Moses and Aaron," as translated in Karl H. Worner, *Schoenberg's 'Moses and Aaron'* (London: Faber and Faber, 1959), pp. 137 & 163.

[5] William F. Lynch, S.J., *Images of Hope* (Baltimore: Helicon, 1967), pp. 177-8.

[6] John W. Dixon, Jr., *Art and the Theological Imagination* (New York: Seabury Press, 1978), p. 96.

[7] Some of this material previously appeared in Thomas G. Long, "Bit Parts in the Christmas Pageant," *Journal for Preachers,* Vol. VI, No. 1 (Advent, 1982), p. 20. It is used by permission.

[8] Dixon, p. 96.

We Interrupt This Service . . .

It was question and answer time at the worship workshop. I had been speaking on the theme of worship all morning to a group of people gathered in a church fellowship hall in a suburban neighborhood in Indiana. Dressed in sweatshirts and jeans, they had given up a Saturday of golf and gardening to sip coffee and listen politely as I rambled through discussions of Vatican II, Calvin's view of the Lord's Supper, the pros and cons of children's sermons, the development of the lectionary, the meanings of baptism, and other assorted topics about worship. Now, the lecturing done, I gulped down a little coffee of my own and asked if there were any questions.

A hand shot into the air. It belonged to a fiftyish man with plump cheeks and rimless glasses who was, judging by the way his hand waved and bobbed, eager to speak. "There's one thing about our worship service here which really gripes me," he complained. "To me it's like fingernails being scraped across a blackboard."

"What's that?" I cautiously asked, fully expecting him to say something about gender inclusive language, new-fangled hymns, politics in the pulpit, or sermons on tithing. But it was not one of these issues which caused his aggravation.

"The announcements," he declared. "I just hate it when the minister spoils the mood of worship with all those dull announcements." Heads bobbed in vigorous agreement all around the room. The announcements were out of favor in that corner of Indiana, no question about it.

I knew what the man meant, of course. You're soaring above the pews on Sunday, your wings catching the strong breeze of the Spirit carrying you upward from "Joy to the World" toward the choir's lofty "For Unto Us a Child is Born," and then, thud . . . "the Christian Education Committee will meet in the library on Thursday at 7:30 . . ." Like Icarus striving for the sun, you find your wax wings suddenly melting, and you plummet back to the world of flesh, dust, and committee meetings.

I know what he meant. The announcements do seem like a bag of peanuts at the opera, an ungainly moment of mundanity wedging its way into an hour of inspiration. What I tried to say to the questioner was that I understood how he felt and that, yes, the announcements were often rattled off without care or passion, and, yes, they did sometimes seem to be somewhat uninspiring, but that, after all, the details of the church's institutional life were *important,* and five minutes of them couldn't hurt, and so on.

In short, I blew it. What I should have said is that, properly understood, the announcements are one of those places where the rubber of the church's theology hits the road. Indeed, it just may be that by moving seamlessly from "Holy, Holy, Holy" to "the telephone crisis counseling ministry is in need of additional volunteers," by punctuating its soaring praise with the commas of the earthy details of its common life, the church is expressing in its worship one of its most basic convictions about the character of God: "The Word became flesh and dwelt among us . . ." (John 1:14)

That affirmation about the eternal Word becoming flesh comes, of course, from the poem which opens the Gospel of John. The poem begins with violins and soaring phrases: "In the beginning was the Word, and the Word was with God, and the Word was God . . ." (John 1:1) With these ethereal phrases at the beginning of John's gospel, it is no wonder that the church selected, as a symbol for John the Evangelist, the high flying eagle. If John's poem had ended after the first line, the noble Greek philosophers could have voiced their admiring approval. They, too, wanted to mount up with eagle's wings, to leave the earth behind, and to ascend into the celestial heights to be with God and his *logos,* his Word.

But John's poem does not end with the first line. The eagle suddenly dives toward the ground. The violins give way to the blunt thud of a bass drum. Heaven crashes to the earth. The closing notes of the hymn fade, and it is time for the first startlingly earth bound announcement in Christian history: "The Word became flesh and dwelt among us . . ." It is here that John and the Greeks part company. The very idea that the ultimate meeting between humanity and the *logos* of God would come, not when we ascended to the airy pinnacle, but when the *logos* descended to the fleshy depths was, to employ the term of New Testament scholar Raymond Brown, "unthinkable," John's poem, Brown says, does not claim . . .

. . . that the Word entered into flesh or abided in flesh but that the Word became *flesh. Therefore, instead of supplying the liberation from the material world that the Greek mind yearned for, the Word of God was now inextricably bound to human history.*[1]

The conviction that God refused to float in sublime isolation above time and space, but became, in Jesus Christ, flesh and blood, sweat and earth, is the doctrine of the incarnation, and what it means, among other things, is that we do not escape the mundane to encounter the living God. Indeed, the announcements in worship become symbolic of the Christian truth that it is the "fleshy" details of life, the working and the serving, the community projects and the committee meetings, the being born, the marrying, and the dying, which are the arenas for our encounter with God-become-flesh in Jesus Christ. When the announcements about soup kitchens, new babies, people in the hospital, Bible studies, and meetings of Alcoholics Anonymous begin, "Holy, Holy, Holy" does not end; the church is simply confessing that *these* are the places

where that holiness is to be found. "The Word became flesh
. . ."

Now the church has always known that affirming this doctrine of the incarnation was like carrying around a lighted stick
of dynamite. On the one hand, it is capable of blasting away
virtually everyone who prefers less fleshy brands of religion.
For those who seek religious experience and inner peace
through the inward path of meditation, for example, there is
John insisting that the path of God does not end in rarified
spirit, but in *flesh*. In other words, however many inward turns
the path may take, it eventually leads out to the world of flesh
where we are called to meet Christ in human community. One
of the telling criticisms of the electronic church is that it also
isolates the viewer from the "fleshiness" of human community. As one observer put it, the television church offers religious experience in the safe and sterile environment of one's
own living room and not among "sniffling children, restless
teenagers, hard-of-hearing grandparents, and sleepy parish-
ioners." Moreover . . .

*. . . When you watch television church, no one asks you to partici-
pate in a visitation program. No one challenges you to hold the attention of a junior high Sunday school class. No one asks you to
take meals to shut-ins.*[2]

In short, it is all pure religion and no messy entanglements
with human flesh. All of which is fine until the old eagle John
swoops to earth with his announcement: "The Word became
flesh . . ."

On the other hand, the doctrine of incarnation blows up
all naive notions of the inherent and natural holiness of life.
It was God who became flesh, not flesh that became God. In
the movie about Saint Francis of Assisi, "Brother Son, Sister
Moon," the birds and all of nature preach their granola fla-
vored goodness to *Francis*. In the church's story, however,
Francis preaches to the *birds,* and therein lies the crucial difference. All of creation was fallen — *all* of it. To use John's

language, darkness was everywhere. In Jesus Christ, God entered creation, became flesh, and all of the darkness in the world cannot overcome the light of that saving act.

The incarnation means that, appearances to the contrary, all of human life and history is infused with holiness, but this does not mean that life is a lark or that we are called to sing as a hymn the words of the popular song, "Everything is beautiful, in its own way." Anyone who has seen the torture chambers of the Nazi regime, any surgeon who has removed a malignant tumor, any reformer who has tried to clean up government, knows that everything is *not* beautiful in its own way. To affirm the incarnation does not imply that life is rosy or that people always do the right thing or even the best they can. It does not mean that people do not waste their lives, get hurt or hurt other people. It does not mean that there is no hardship, no drudgery, no evil, no tragedy. It would be an illusion to pretend otherwise. What it does mean is that there is no corner of experience so hidden that grace cannot find it. There is no soil so sterile that the seed of holy wonder cannot grow in it. There is no moment so dark that it can extinguish the light of God which even now shines in it. Christians do not bubble around celebrating life. They celebrate God who enters the life of creation in order to redeem it. "The Word became flesh . . ."

When Christians say, "The Word became flesh and dwelt among us, full of grace and truth," they do not mean that God *is* everything, but they do mean that God is *in* everything. "In everything," wrote Paul to the Romans, "God works for good with those who love him . . ."(Romans 8:28) The theologian Robert McAfee Brown likes to use in his writing the musical metaphor of themes and variations.[3] There are many musical compositions, Beethoven's "Fifth Symphony" for example, which begin with a clear, identifiable musical pattern, or theme. What follows in the music is a series of variations on this theme, the theme being repeated in ever more complex combinations. Sometimes the texture of these combinations is so complex that the theme is hidden, seemingly obscured by the competing and interlocking notes. But those who have heard the theme clearly stated at the beginning of the work can still make it out, can feel the music being organized by the theme. In Jesus Christ "the Word became flesh and dwelt among us, full of grace and truth . . ." That's the theme of all of life heard clearly by the ears of faith, and those who have heard that distinct theme can hear it being sounded wherever the music of life is being played, no matter how jangled are the false notes surrounding it.

In her book *Pilgrim at Tinker Creek,* Annie Dillard told about seeing a mockingbird dive straight down off the roof of a four-story building. "It was an act as careless and spontaneous as the curl of a stem . . ." she wrote. The mockingbird, wings held tightly against its body, descending at thirty-two feet per second toward the earth, spread his wings at the last possible second and floated onto the ground. Dillard said she spotted this amazing display just as she rounded a corner. No one else was there to witness it. She connected the event to the old philosophical question about the tree falling in the forest. If no one were there to hear it, goes the conundrum, would it make a sound? "The answer must be," she stated

> . . . I think, that beauty and grace are performed whether or not we will sense them. The least we can do is try to be there.[4]

Because in Jesus Christ the Word became flesh, truth and grace are at work in every place, whether or not we sense them. What we can do, of course, is to attempt to master the theme and then to try to be there wherever in life it is played anew. If we wonder where that might be, one good place to begin is by listening in worship to the announcements.

58

Notes

[1] Raymond E. Brown, *The Gospel According to John (I-XII) [The Anchor Bible,* Vol. 29]* (Garden City, New York: Doubleday and Company, 1966), p. 31.

[2] Philip Yancey, *Open Windows* (Nashville: Thomas Nelson Publishers, 1985), p. 73.

[3] See, for example, chapter eighteen in Robert McAfee Brown, *The Bible Speaks to You* (Philadelphia: The Westminster Press, 1955), pp. 231 ff.

[4] Annie Dillard, *The Pilgrim at Tinker Creek,* as quoted in Yancey, p. 24.

Mark 1:4-11 (C, L)
Mark 1:7-11 (RC)

The Baptism of Our Lord
(Epiphany 1)

Knowing the Secret

One of the decisions every good storyteller has to make is when to tell the story's secret to people. Every story has a secret, and the spinner of tales has to decide whether to let them know about the secret early in the story or to surprise them with it at the end. Mystery writers often hold back the secret until the last chapter, keeping us eagerly turning the pages to discover who really poisoned the heiress or pushed Colonel Whitington down the elevator shaft. The same is true of soap operas. "Will Marletta find true happiness with Jason the chauffeur?" the old radio announcers would intone. "Tune in tomorrow for the next episode of 'The Bright Horizon.' " In other words, turn the next page, tune in tomorrow, and you'll learn the secret.

There are other stories, however, in which the storyteller reveals the secret at the beginning. We know the secret even before some of the characters do, and we watch them gradually discover the hidden truth we already possess. "Oh Grandma, what big eyes you have," trills the innocent Little Red Riding Hood. But we already know, don't we, the secret of what ravenous destruction lies bonnet-clad under those covers. Or, in another children's tale, the "ugly duckling," shunned because of his homeliness, finally emerges as the lovely swan we knew him to be all along.

In Princeton, New Jersey, there is a legendary tale about the eminent scientist Albert Einstein walking in front of a local inn and being mistaken for a bell boy by a dowager who had just arrived in a luxury sedan. She orders him to carry her luggage into the hotel, and, according to the story, Einstein does so, receives a small tip, and then continues on to his office to ponder the mysteries of the universe. True or not, the story is delightful, precisely because we savor from the beginning a secret the dowager does not know: the strange-looking, ruffled little man is the most celebrated intellect of our time. Some stories gain their power from our knowing the story's secret from the start.

The Gospel of Mark is just such a story. The secret of Mark's gospel is the identity of Jesus Christ. In the very first sentence of the gospel story, Mark lifts the veil and lets us know the secret when he says that this is ". . . the gospel of Jesus Christ, the Son of God." Jesus is the Son of God, that's the secret, and lest we miss it, this hidden truth is confirmed in the story's opening episode, when Jesus, coming up out of the waters of baptism, sees the Holy Spirit descending upon him like a dove from the heavens, which have been torn open like a piece of cloth, and hears the very voice of God telling the secret: "Thou art my beloved Son; with thee I am well pleased." (Mark 1:11) Only Jesus sees the Spirit; only Jesus hears the voice. This is, in the words of one commentator, "a secret epiphany."[1]

God knows the secret. Now Jesus knows the secret. And, because Mark has let us in on it, we know the secret, too. Jesus is the Son of God. And now we watch with amazement as the story unfolds, because almost no one else seems to be able to discover the secret. The authorities mistake him for a troublemaker; the people confuse him with the prophet Elijah among others; even his disciples are blind to the full truth of who he is. Ironically, in the middle of the story only the demons he has come to destroy recognize the secret that Jesus is the Son of God. The thing is, he doesn't *look* like the Son of God. Like the genius Einstein dragging the heavy suitcases of a wealthy woman up the steps of a hotel, Jesus does not look like who he really is. That's part of the reason the secret remains hidden. Why doesn't Jesus look like the Son of God? Because he suffers, and *that* seems unlikely in God's own son. Jesus is the *suffering* Son of God, and that is a hard secret to learn.

Once the disciples came very near to discovering the secret.

"Who do you say that I am?" Jesus asked them.

Peter stepped forward to answer, "You are the Christ." Does Peter know the secret? No, because Jesus immediately began to tell them the whole secret, that he faced suffering, rejection, and death, and Peter rebuked him. Peter does not really understand the secret. Jesus is the *suffering* Son of God, and that is a hard secret to learn.

That is why Mark tells us the secret in the beginning. He wants us to know that Jesus is the Son of God when all hell breaks loose on Golgotha. No reasonable person who takes one look at this pitiable Galilean dragging the luggage of the world's scorn up the steps of Calvary would say, "This is the Son of God," but Mark wants us to remember the secret. When the most devout people of his day spit in Jesus' face and called him "blasphemer," Mark wants us to remember the secret. When the Roman soldiers turned his trial into a fraternity party, dressing him in a purple blanket and a crown of thorns, holding their sides with cruel laughter as they knelt before him in mock respect, Mark wants us to remember the secret. When they drove the spikes into his flesh and taunted him to come down from the cross, Mark wants us to remember the secret. There at the end, with the sky murderously dark, the air filled with Jesus' death cry, and the temple curtain torn in two, Mark wants us to remember that earlier day when the skies, like the temple curtain, were also torn in two and a voice spoke from heaven. Mark wants us to hear the centurion at the foot of the cross confessing the secret we have known from the beginning, "Truly this man was the Son of God!"

Appearance and reality — that's the meaning of Mark's secret. The one who appeared to be rejected is in reality the one in whom God is well-pleased. The one who appeared to be deserted by all is in reality the beloved Son. The one who appeared impotent in death is the one in whose power all shall live. That's the secret revealed in the baptism of Jesus, and it is the secret in which all Christians share through baptism.

In Flannery O'Conner's story "The River," a woman named Mrs. Connin, who has been employed for the day to take care of the son of some wealthy and uncaring parents, takes the boy to a riverside baptismal service being led by a preacher named Bevel Summers. Standing on the river bank, they hear Summers warning the crowd that if they have come for an easy miracle, to leave their pain in the river, they have come for the wrong reason. "There ain't but one river, and that's the River of Life, made out of Jesus' blood," he says. "It's a river of pain itself . . . to be washed away, slow, you people, slow . . ." Suddenly Mrs. Connin lifted the boy up in the air and asks the preacher to pray for the boy's mother, who has been ill. Mrs. Connin tells Summers that she suspects that the boy has never been baptized, and Summers commands her to hand the boy to him. Summers asks the boy if he wants to be baptized. When the boy says yes, Summers responds, "You won't be the same again. You'll count."[2]

Appearance and reality. In the baptism of Jesus the secret of his identity is revealed and nothing that appears thereafter, not even the spit and nails of Golgotha, can take that reality away. In our baptism the secret of our identity is revealed: "You are a child of God. You won't be the same again. You'll count." And nothing that appears thereafter can take that reality away. "For in Christ Jesus," writes Paul in Galatians, "you are all children of God, through faith. For as many of you who were baptized into Christ have put on Christ." (Galatians 3:26-27)

Doc is a character in John Steinbeck's *Sweet Thursday*. A Ph.D from the University of Chicago, Doc now earns his living selling marine specimens he has collected from the tidal pools near his home in Monterey. He has a good life, but when he reflects deeply, Doc is troubled by a nagging sense of discontent. "Have I worked enough? Have I eaten enough? Have I loved enough? . . . What has my life meant so far, and what can it mean in the time left to me? . . . What have I contributed to the Great Ledger? What am I worth?"[3]

What am I worth? For many, life unfolds, day after day, with the question unanswered, the verdict in suspense. Have I worked enough? Have I loved enough? What am I worth? The secret remains hidden to the end, the truth never really known.

"When I consider the briefness of my life," mused Pascal, "swallowed up before and behind it, the small space I fill, or even see, engulfed in the infinite immensity of spaces which I know not, and which know not me, I am afraid

. . . Who has set me here? By whose order and arrangement have this place and time been allotted to me?'' For many, the secret remains concealed. Who am I? Why am I here? What am I worth? I am afraid.

In baptism the secret is out at the beginning, the truth is known at the inception, and there is no need to fear, come what may. "You are my beloved child, my very own. I have placed you here and called you to be my own. In you I delight."

In his autobiographical book *Creative Dislocation,* Robert McAfee Brown remembered the day in 1960 when he participated in a Lutheran worship service in East Berlin, only a short time before the Berlin Wall was constructed. There were not many people present, for church attendance was viewed with suspicion by the state. The East German Republic had developed secular alternatives to replace all of the rituals of the church. Nonetheless, a young couple are there in the service, presenting their child for baptism, and Brown was amazed. Why, he wondered, would they jeopardize their future and that of their child by insisting on this ancient ritual of baptism when a secular alternative was readily and painlessly available? Brown wrote:

> *The couple does not have to answer my question. Their very act of bringing their baby to the church is a public statement of their priorities. They engage in significant risk because of their faith. In the face of their quiet, public courage I feel unworthy.*[4]

This couple knew a secret about their child which no secular tyranny could take away: this is a child of God. The secret of the story is let out at the beginning, and nothing in all creation, neither death nor life nor things present nor things to come, can change the story. This is a child of God, baptized in the very name of the one whose secret we have always known: Surely this is the Son of God!

Notes

[1] Lamar Williamson, Jr., *Mark* [Interpretation Commentaries] (Atlanta: John Knox Press, 1983), p. 35.

[2] Flannery O'Conner, "The River" in *The Complete Stories* (New York: Farrar, Straus, and Giroux, 1971), pp. 165-6.

[3] John Steinbeck, *Sweet Thursday* as quoted in Robert McAfee Brown, *Creative Dislocation* (Nashville: Abingdon Press, 1980), p. 118.

[4] Robert McAfee Brown, *Creative Dislocation* (Nashville: Abingdon Press, 1980), p. 19.

Party in Room 210 . . . Everyone Invited

William Muehl has a bone to pick with ministers. Muehl is on the faculty of Yale Divinity School, and he has spent many years teaching people who are about to become ministers and those who are already ministers. William Muehl is well acquainted with ministers, and he has a complaint.

What bothers Professor Muehl is what he sees as a widespread tendency among ministers to do some romantic editorial work on the nature of Christian calling. To hear most ministers talk, claims Muehl, God calls people only in moments of theatrical intensity. Someone, for example, is reading a theological book when, suddenly, a shaft of light falls upon a penetrating passage and scales fall from the reader's eyes. Or a hillside communion service at a summer church camp begins to glow with all the luminosity and power of the Upper Room. The ministerial version of Christian calling almost always involves a moment of high drama.

Muehl does not doubt that such moments do occur, but he *does* doubt that they occur as often and as predictably as some ministers say they do. Muehl thinks many ministers are guilty of dressing up these events in "Damascus Road" garb, which is unfortunate since most people come to faith, he says, in ways that are far more gritty and down-to-earth. They were forced into Sunday church school by their parents, or found the local church youth group to be a reliable way to spice up an otherwise dull weekend, or discovered that the sanctuary could be entered on the arm of an attractive member of the opposite sex. "These ways seem . . . to have at least one thing in common," states Muehl. "They are not nearly as dramatic and intellectually impressive as people feel a genuine religious experience ought to be."[1]

One of the reasons which prompts Muehl to complain is his own experience of call. He was trained as an attorney and discovered, in the law school's moot court, that he was an exceptionally effective trial lawyer. He won his cases, for the most part, but the emotional stress of doing so caused him to develop a duodenal ulcer. After treating him for several gastric episodes, one of the health service physicians made a dire prediction. "Muehl," he said, "if you really undertake a career in the law, you will probably be rich by the age of forty. The only trouble is that you will be *dead* by the age of thirty."

Hearing this, Muehl left the field of law and joined the faculty of Yale Divinity School. Surrounded there by colleagues who had come to their work in response to a genuine sense of calling, Muehl soon began to doubt that he had experienced a real call, so he approached another faculty member, the ethicist H. Richard Niebuhr, with his concern. Niebuhr puffed on his pipe, laughed gently, and responded, "What does it take to make up a 'call' for you, Muehl? What you had planned to do with your life was quite literally eating you up inside, driving you . . . to consider alternatives. I can't imagine a better call outside the Bible."[2]

What does it take to make up a "call" for you? That's an intriguing question, and one which lies at the heart of today's passage from the Gospel of John. At first glance, this text would seem to work against Muehl's conviction that Christian calling occurs in everyday prose rather than in theological poetry. John the Baptizer is standing with two of his disciples when Jesus happens by. Using language which sounds more like the poetry of the liturgy than it does the prose of the street, John points dramatically to Jesus, "Behold, the Lamb of God!" Seemingly moved by the compelling mystery of the moment, the two disciples follow Jesus. In terms of the question, What does it take to make up a call?, at this point the score seems to be: poetry 1, prose O.

But if we look closely at the rest of the passage, the story begins to speak of other, more prosaic and earth-bound realities. To be sure, the two disciples of John do follow Jesus, but they do not seem to be fully certain of what they are doing. When Jesus notices that they are following him, he asks them, "What do you seek?," or, to put it more directly, "Do you know what you're looking for when you follow me?"

The pair answer Jesus, not with a confident statement of discipleship, but with another question. "Rabbi, where are you staying?" Now this is a strange response. Jesus asks them a question about discipleship; they counter with an inquiry about his housing situation. Biblical scholars know, however, that this is a question not merely about lodging, but about the nature of Jesus himself. "Where are you staying?" means, in essence, "Who are you? Where is the 'home,' the center of your life?" It would not be stretching things to translate the disciples' response as, "At this point we don't know whom we are following or where this path is leading. Can you tell us?"

Jesus then invites them to "come and see," and it is only in the journeying and in the seeing that they begin to fathom the true dimensions of what is happening to them.

The story goes on to tell us that one of these disciples was Andrew, the brother of a man named Simon. Andrew goes to his brother and tells him, "We have found the Christ," and then Andrew brings Simon to Jesus.

Jesus takes one look at Simon and then says, in what surely must have been a startling statement, "So you are Simon. I'm changing your name. From now on, you will be called 'Peter.' "

What does it take to make up a "call"? The picture John gives us, when we inspect it closely, now seems closer to the gritty and ambiguous realities of life. We see people stumbling along, following a presence they do not yet understand, discovering only belatedly and after the fact that the path they have ventured upon has led to the Christ. We see a portrait of a person being tugged along to Jesus by a brother, following more out of family loyalty perhaps than out of a sense of mystery, finding at the end of the trail, and not at the beginning, that his name . . . and his life . . . have been transformed.

All of this goes to make Muehl's basic point: "The roads to Christian faith are as varied as the people who profess it."[3] There in the congregation is the man who would rather be sitting in the car in the church parking lot reading the sports page of the Sunday paper were it not for the fact that his wife has insisted that he put on a suit and tie and accompany her into the sanctuary. There also is the teenager in the balcony with one ear on the pastoral prayer and the other focused on the whispers of her boyfriend. There is the couple who have come because they were invited by the family across the street and they had no handy excuse not to say yes. There is the young woman who is there because of the music and who reads the hymnbook during the sermon.

The point of all this is that the calling to follow Christ is a pathway which is marked "come and see." It is a pathway which is far more important because of where it leads than because of where it begins. It may begin, as it did for Muehl, as a pain in the body, or, as it has for others, as a longing in the heart, a struggle in the soul, or a wondering in the mind. It is a path which some people enter alone, which others enter by tagging along with friends or family, and down which yet others are dragged, at first reluctantly, by parents or teachers. No matter how we begin, we see as we travel that the pathway has been cleared for us by the Christ who goes before us, making of our many beginnings a common journey. "Come and see," we are told, though the voice which calls us sometimes seems faint, filtered through the voices of the ordinary folk around us. And, for whatever reason, we *do* go, and, then, we *do* see. What we see is that, no matter who we were when we started, we end up with a new name, a new identity, given by Christ. What we see is that, no matter how we began our travel, we end the journey resting in the Christ who is all in all.

There is a woman I know who began her journey in faith because she loved to sing. To put it more bluntly, she loved to sing in front of other people, and she warmed to the lavish compliments and enthusiastic responses generated by her lovely voice. The local church choir was not exactly show business, but it was as close to that as she could come, so she sang there. The rest of the worship was of no interest to her, and she would often secretly read a paperback novel in the choir loft, waiting her chance to perform.

Then, somehow, the words of the solos and the anthems began to have a certain power for her. "Worthy is the lamb who was slain," and "I know that my Redeemer liveth," began to speak to her beyond the concerns of musical phrasing and pitch. She was gradually acquiring not only an acquaintance with the vocabulary of the faith, but also a relationship to the One to whom those words point. Now, when she sings, she does so with a new name. She is no longer "performer." She is "witness."

What does it take to make up a "call"? Perhaps every church ought to paint the words "come and see" over the doorway, and give to everyone who enters, for whatever reason, a joyful word of welcome and a knapsack for the journey ahead.

I was once staying in a motel in a large city and was surprised to find, posted to the elevator door, a small, handwritten notice which read, "Party tonight! Room 210. 8:00 p.m. Everyone invited!" I could hardly picture who would throw such a party, or for what reason, but I imagined that at eight o'clock, room 210 would be filled by an unlikely assortment of people — sales representatives seeking a little relief from the tedium of the road; a vacationing couple tired of sightseeing; a man stopping overnight in the middle of a long journey,

looking for a bit of festivity; a few inquisitive and wary motel employees, there because of professional responsibility; perhaps some young people who had slipped out of their parents' rooms, anxiously curious about what was happening in room 210.

Alas, the sign by the elevator soon came down, replaced by a typewritten statement from the motel staff explaining that the original notice was a hoax, a practical joke. That made sense, of course, but in a way it was too bad. For a brief moment, those of us staying at the motel were tantalized by the possibility that there just might be a party going on somewhere to which we were all invited — a party where it didn't make much difference who we were when we walked in the door, or what motivated us to come; a party we could come to out of boredom, loneliness, curiosity, responsibility, eagerness to be in fellowship, or simply out of a desire to come and see what was happening; a party where it didn't matter nearly as much what got us in the door, as what would happen to us after we arrived.

Perhaps if there is to be such a party, the church is going to have to throw it.

Notes

[1] William Muehl, *Why Preach? Why Listen?* (Philadelphia: Fortress Press, 1986), p. 17.

[2] *Ibid.,* pp. 18-19.

[3] *Ibid.,* p. 17.

What Do You See?

It was a rollicking night at the theater. A young actor named Tom Key was playing the part of Jesus in the play *Cotton Patch Gospel* and he was clearly bringing the house down. The play, a romping, bluegrass musical which depicts the ministry of Jesus as if it had occurred in the cotton fields and Baptist churches of rural south Georgia, was in its final performance run, and Key was feeling confident and even inventive with his lines. His spontaneous enthusiasm was contagious, and he had forged between himself and the audience a rare bond of mutual exchange and appreciation.

During the scene depicting the Sermon on the Mount, Key, as Jesus, suddenly turned from the group on the stage toward the audience, pointed to the blank auditorium side wall, and said, "Look at the lilies in that field . . ." He stopped, almost as if he had forgotten the next line, peered around at the disciples, focused again on the audience and repeated, "*Look* at the lilies in that field . . ." Once more he stopped and seemed to be searching for the next words. The audience began to shift uncomfortably. His hand extended yet again to the blank wall, and this time he spoke the words slowly and deliberately, "*Look* . . . at . . . the . . .lilies . . . in . . . that . . . field . . ." Now he turned to the disciples, shrugging his shoulders, and said, "I can't get them to look." The room filled with laughter as it dawned on the audience that he *really* wanted us to look. And sure enough, when he gave one more try,

"*Look* at the lilies in that field . . ." every head in the audience turned toward the side wall.

I do not know whether old John the Evangelist was present in the theater that night, but, if not, he should have been. It was his kind of show. Indeed, he spends his entire gospel trying to get people to look, really to *look,* at the life of Jesus. Light and darkness, vision and dimness, "once I was blind, but now I see," these are the materials of John's gospel. Chapter after chapter, John's finger points toward his Lord and his voice sounds the refrain, "Look . . . look . . . look."

The willingness to look and to see stands at the center of this story about Nathaniel. According to John, Nathaniel is approached by Philip, who tells Nathaniel that they have found the one Moses and the prophets wrote about, and his name is Jesus of Nazareth. Nathaniel crosses his arms, closes his eyes, and plays the pre-recorded tape of a blind prejudice which sees nothing but knows everything, "Can anything good come out of Nazareth?"

Philip responds with three words which embrace everything the church knows to say in its evangelism: "Come and see." Like children who have seen a meteor shower lighting up the night sky and have run breathlessly into the house to beckon their parents, the church runs toward the world, pulling it gently but urgently by the hand, "Come and see. Come and see. There are wonders beyond imagining to behold."

"Come and see," says John's gospel, but the actor playing Jesus, shrugging his shoulders, said, "I can't get them to look." Sometimes people do not see the grace at work in the world through Christ because they will not *come* to the place where they can see. The light shines in the darkness, and the darkness has not overcome it, but the light is not visible from every vantage point. One must *come* and see.

A few years ago a church located in a large city decided to turn its gymnasium into a night shelter for homeless people. Every winter there were reports that some of these people, condemned to sleep out in the open, had frozen to death, and so the church made the warmth and safety of its building available without charge. Each evening during the winter, volunteers from the church would spend the night in the shelter, providing food, clothing, and lodging for as many of the homeless as the building would hold. Almost without exception, the volunteers reported that the experience of spending the night with these people from the streets had been far more than an act of dutiful charity. The volunteers had found their own faith strengthened, their own reliance upon the grace of Christ reinforced by the experience.

Several months after the shelter was opened, one of the pastors of the church was being interviewed on a radio talk program. The interviewer was an opinionated fundamentalist whose biases were quite strong. It became clear during the interview that he felt that the church ought to stick to the business of preaching the old-time gospel and stay away from meddlesome activities like shelters for homeless people. "Now just tell me," he jeered at one point, "where is *Jesus* in all this?" For a moment the pastor considered silently how to respond, then said calmly, "You just have to *be* there."

"Come and see," said Philip to Nathaniel, and some people do not see because they will not come to those places where one can get an angle of vision, where one can see the grace of Christ at work in the world.

"Come and see," calls John's gospel, but the Jesus of the "Cotton Patch Gospel" shrugged his shoulders and said, "I can't get them to look." There are other times when people do not see the grace at work in the world through Christ, because, even when they come to the place where Christ is at work, they will not *look* . . .really look. Like bored tourists in an art museum, they glance at everything but see nothing . . .

• worship becomes a "nice ceremony" full of pleasant music and sweet-sounding words rather than the arena for encountering the living God.

• marriage becomes a contract between self-seeking partners, rather than a place of holy intimacy.

• sex becomes the warm cuddling of mutual gratification,
devoid of all mystery.

• human striving toward freedom and dignity becomes
"merely political," rather than a sign of God at work in the
world breaking all forms of bondage.

Some peer at everything, but see nothing.

Come and see. In some ways, this is all that can be said
to us . . . all that needs to be said to us. Nathaniel went, and
Nathaniel saw. Jesus gave him new eyes, and with them he
saw the true light. "Rabbi," he exclaimed, "you are the Son
of God!" To which Jesus replied, in effect, "Keep looking,
Nathaniel. There's evenmore to see." If we do come with a
willingness to see, then, like Nathaniel, we will find a Christ
who will open our blind eyes, clear the dimness of our vision,
and show us more wonders of grace than we ever dreamed were
there to see.

In her book *Becoming Human,* Letty M. Russell, describes
the new sense of vision which was given to her, ironically, when
she lost one of her eyes in a freak accident. Things which had
once loomed large for her now became small in the light of
the more important realities of sight, health, and the compas-
sionate care of others. Moreover, her personal pain heightened
her sensitivity to the pain of others and deepened her awareness of her own need for God's care. In other words, though
she had lost an eye, she could *see more.* She wrote:

> *This discovery that I was becoming at one and the same time*
> *both stronger and weaker was a small sign that God was pa-*
> *tiently helping me to become more human.*[1]

In a certain church in the midwest, the officers were

debating whether to join several other churches in their sponsorship of a local family health clinic. The clinic had been established for the families of migrant workers because the public health resources were inadequate and burdened with red tape. In the debate one of the officers spoke forcefully against supporting the clinic because, as he put it, "Most of the patients are illegal aliens, so we'd just be supporting illegal activity."

"But they're *people,*" said another in the group, "and they need medical care." Back and forth went the discussion, with much passion but without resolution. Taking a vote would have been bitterly divisive, so the matter was tabled until the next meeting.

On the following day, the pastor of the church called the officer who had spoken in opposition and made a date for lunch. During lunch the pastor asked him if he would be willing to take a few minutes on the way back to work and visit the clinic in question. The man agreed, and the two of them found the waiting room at the clinic bustling with activity, full of pensive young mothers and squirming children. The pastor and the man sat down to observe for a few minutes.

A nurse appeared at the door and called to one of the children, a little boy, about four years old, who marched bravely toward the nurse, already apprehensively rubbing his arm where he knew he would soon receive an innoculation.

A few minutes later the little boy reappeared at the door, now rubbing his pained arm in earnest, poking his lower lip forward, fighting the tears that were pushing out of his eyes. He searched the room for his mother, but she had taken another child to the restroom and was not to be found. The boy, finding what looked to him like a kind face, walked over to the man, crawled onto his lap, and rested his head on the man's chest.

First hesitantly, then willingly and lovingly, the man wrapped his hands around this fellow human being in need of care. When he did so, he was amazed by his own spontaneous compassion. Almost as amazed as were the other officers when he made the motion at the next meeting to sponsor the clinic.

"Come and see," said Philip to Nathaniel. And what did he see? . . . Well, you just have to be there.

Notes

[1] Letty M. Russell, *Becoming Human* (Philadelphia: Westminster Press, 1982), p. 103.

Mark 1:14-20   *Epiphany 3 (C, L)*
                                       Ordinary Time 3 (RC)

Hot Tubs and Fishing Trips

The following classified advertisement appeared in a recent edition of a major city newspaper:

HOT TUB — For sale, complete w/plumbing. Will trade for
pick-up truck. Call _____ after 5:00 p.m.

One does not have to possess a Ph.D. in clinical psychology
to suspect that, behind those few words, there lies a life in
major transition. Away with the hot tub, the gold chains, the
Brut, the Alfa Romeo, the wine coolers, and the avocado dip.
In with the baseball cap, the Budweiser, the flannel shirt, the
Old Spice, and the Chevy half-ton.

One also does not have to be trained in sociology to recognize that we live in a culture rife with these kinds of transfor-
mations, what are sometimes called "lifestyle changes." People
all across the map are becoming vegetarians, signing up for
"marriage encounter" weekends, taking up jogging or sail-
ing, leaving their spouses, changing careers, entering "mid-
life crises," trying to become "computer literate," working
on new relationships, giving up alcohol, "getting into" ther-
apy, joining prayer groups, learning to be more assertive, and
making scores of other adjustments to the compass settings
of their life journeys.

It is easy to be cynical, of course, about such changes. Many of them are faddishly superficial, containing more conformity than conversion, the kind of chic skittering around the pampered and affluent landscape of pop culture so roundly satirized by Cyra McFadden in her novel *The Serial*. The book is set in a laid-back, fern-bar-saturated community of beautiful people, all of them frantically fine-tuning their social styles to the rapidly changing *zeitgeist*. For example, two of the characters plan a party around the renewal of their marriage "contract" and send the following invitation to their friends:

> *Kate Smith and Harvey Holroyd*
> *request your presence*
> *at a Spring Festival —*
> *a Celebration of Open Commitment and*
> *Feeling Exchange where we can just* Be.
> *Come reaffirm with us our belief*
> *that in Life, it's the Journay that counts,*
> *not the Goal.*[1]

However well-aimed such parody may be, it is not the whole story. It is true that many of our attempts at change are laughably naive and shallow, but taken as markers of the human condition, they also point to a deeper restlessness, a more urgent quest. However silly or trivial they may appear on the surface, the changes people make in their lives are often signs of a crucial, frequently desperate, sometimes courageous, search. If that is true, what is it that we are searching *for?* What is it that causes people to contemplate important changes in their lives? What motivates them to leave a place of settled circumstances and values and venture off into a new and uncharted region?

Some of the shifts people make in their lives are simply rebellions against boredom. They are not planned trips to a new destination,; they are simply tickets on the first bus out of town. In Herb Gardner's play *A Thousand Clowns,* Murray Burns, an open-collared, disorganized, and voluntarily unemployed free spirit, is explaining to Arnold, his disciplined and socially conventional brother, that it was the fear of numbing boredom which drove him to abandon the traditional "nine to five" life:

> *Arnold five months ago I forgot what* day *it was. I'm on the* subway on my way to work and I didn't know what day it *was . . . for a minute it could have been* any *day . . . Arnie, it scared the hell out of me.*[2]

Another playwright, Arthur Miller, stated it this way in an essay:

> *People no longer seem to know why they are alive; existence is simply a string of near-experiences marked off by periods of stupefying spiritual and psychological stasis, and the good life is basically an amused one.*[3]

Many people, however, have grown weary of making changes simply to alleviate their boredom. They have discovered that the problem with shaking the dust of boredom off one's feet and heading out the door to who knows where, is that leaving one place always means arriving at another place much like the first. One eventually has to show up somewhere else, and that new place is likely to prove as tedium-filled as the last.

This points to another reason why people make important changes in their lives: not so much to get away from a place of boredom, but rather to find a new place of greater meaning. This is not the kind of change in which a person simply heads out the door, slamming it on the way, but the kind in which a person yearns to become a citizen of a new and richer land. It is not a rebellion again boredom; it is a hunger to discover one's true self.

In an interview, Garrison Keillor, the host of public radio's "A Prairie Home Companion," talked about his son, who was at the time fifteen years old. He said that his son had taken up the electric guitar and that his music tended toward the "heavy-metal blues" variety. When Keillor was working at home, writing at the typewriter downstairs, he could hear his son playing, and what he heard amazed him, because the music was so full of *soul* and was "so wrenchingly sad." Keillor went on to wonder about the source of his son's anguish:

> *Where did he learn that? I give him enough money. I'm a nice dad. We get along well. I give him lots of things. He does well in school . . . Where's he get this anguish? I guess we all got it inside of us.*[4]

"We all got it inside of us," and because we do, we are willing to leave the land of anguish in favor of a beckoning land of peace and meaning. Personal or religious renewals are often changes of this sort. As some of the singers in Bernstein's *Mass* express it:

> *What I need I don't have*
> *What I have I don't own*
> *What I own I don't want*
> *What I want, Lord, I don't know . . .*
>
> *What I say I don't feel*
> *What I feel I don't show*
> *What I show isn't real*
> *What is real, Lord — I don't know . . .*[5]

When life is as confusing and disorienting as a ball bouncing in a wildly spinning Roulette wheel, we are eager for it to come to rest on a number, any number, as long as it promises a framework of identity and meaning, be it losing ourselves in work or finding ourselves in God.

The problem with this kind of change is that when we go looking to "find ourselves," we often find ourselves alone. There is a sadness in a culture like ours, which bravely trumpets the virtue of inner-directed, risk-taking, self-sufficient people who don't need anybody else in order to be fully human,

and which, at the same time is full of achingly lonely people.
"Let go . . . Let the changes," goes the bad-medicine prescription of Gail Sheehy in *Passages:*

> *Away from institutional claims and other people's agenda.
> Away from external valuations and accreditations, in search
> of an inner validation. You are moving out of roles and into
> the self.* [6]

And so, people do "let go" and "let the changes." People make courageous changes in their lives trying to "get their act together," only to make the bitter discovery that they have written themselves into the starring role in a one-person play with no audience.

One of the sociologists who authored the book *Habits of the Heart* reported the following interview with a professional woman in her early thirties:

> *Q: So what are you responsible for?*
> A: I'm responsible for my acts and for what I do.
> *Q: Does that mean you're responsible for others, too?*
> A: No.
> *Q: Are you your sister's keeper?*
> A: No.
> *Q: Your brother's keeper?*
> A: No.
> *Q: Are you responsible for your husband?*
> A: I'm not. He makes his own decisions. He is his own
>   person.

It is a worthy goal, I suppose, to want to "be one's own person." No one wants to be pushed around, overwhelmed, and controlled by the demands of others. But there is a deeper sense in which none of us finally wants to "be our own person." We long to hear the sound of another's voice summoning us, valuing our life enough to make a claim upon it. Sometimes, when parents are scolding their children for unacceptable behavior, they will say, "That was *uncalled* for!" That is a strange phrase, when you think of it, "uncalled for," but it points, I believe, to the source of our restless searching and of our most gripping fear. There is a dread in our hearts deeper than the fear of boredom, greater than the anxiety that we will not forge a satisfying "self," and that is the fear that we will ultimately be "uncalled for." This is the fear that no one will ever turn to us and say, "Come, I want *you*. I need *you*." This is the fear that who we are, and what we say, and what we do does not matter to anyone else. Like neighborhood children choosing up sides for a game, each desperately worried about being the last one reluctantly chosen, we make most of the changes in our lives in an effort to make ourselves desirable enough to be summoned by another.

In this light, the story of Jesus passing along the sea, calling Simon and Andrew, James and John, promising to send them "fishing for people," is a moment of sheer wonder and grace. We are told nothing about the inner life of these men. We do not know if they were restless or tranquil, bored or satisfied. What is important is not what was going on *in* them, but what happened *to* them. And what happened to them was this: They were called for. It was a call bigger than self, broader than occupation, deeper even than family. It was a call from the Son of God himself. They were not called for because they had somehow made themselves desirable or competent. They were called for because it is the very life of God to call his people. "Follow me," said Jesus, "and I will send you calling, too." What happened, of course, was that they made the most profound change a person can possibly make: "Immediately, they . . . followed him."

There is a moving scene near the end of Jean Anouilh's play Becket. The King had appointed *Becket,* his old hunting companion and carousing partner, as Archbishop, and then expected Becket to cooperate in a scheme to bring the church under royal control. What the King had not counted on, however, was that Becket would view his ordination as a

82

genuine call, a summons to serve "the honor of God." Becket, therefore, refuses to capitulate to the King's plan. The King is astonished and, reminding Becket of their wild days together at the hunts and in the brothels, claims that this new stance of resistance is not like Becket. "Perhaps." responds Becket. "I am no longer like myself." When the King presses for a reason, Becket describes the sense of call, the feeling that an ultimate claim had been placed on his life, at the time of his ordination:

> *I felt for the first time that I was being entrusted with something, that's all — there in that empty cathedral . . . that day when you ordered me to take up this burden. I was a man without honor And suddenly I found it . . . the honor of God.*[8]

I felt for the first time that I was being entrusted with something. . . "Follow me," said Jesus, "and I will send you fishing in my name." That same summons comes to all of us. For some of us it will come as a call to leave our nets, our books, our desks, our homes. For others it will come as a call to mend our nets more carefully, read our books more thoroughly, mind our desks more faithfully, live in our homes more lovingly. But in whatever form, it has come and will continue to come, the summons to forsake being our "own person" and to become Christ's. And when we hear it, we can be sure that the One who loves us best, and cherishes our life most fully, has come near, and, in the deepest of all ways, we have been called for.

Notes

[1] Cyra McFadden, *The Serial: A Year in the Life of Marin County* (New York: The New American Library, 1977), p. 314.

[2] Herb Gardner, *A Thousand Clowns; Thieves; The Goodbye People* (Garden City, New York: Nelson Doubleday, 1979), pp. 84-5.

[3] Arthur Miller, "The Bored and the Violent," *Harper's Magazine,* Vol. 225, No. 1350 (November, 1962), p. 51.

[4] "Door Interview: Garrison Keillor," *The Wittenberg Door,* No. 82 (December/January 1985), p. 19.

[5] From the libretto of "Mass," words by Stephen Schwartz and Leonard Bernstein. Columbia phonograph recording, Number M2 31008.

[6] Gail Sheehy, *Passages: Predictable Crises of Adult Life* (New York: Bantam Books, 1977), p. 364.

[7] Robert N. Bellah *et al., Habits of the Heart: Individualism and Commitment in American Life* (Berkeley: University of California Press, 1985), p. 304.

[8] Jean Anouilh, *Becket, or the Honor of God* (New York: Coward, McCann, and Geoghegan, 1960), p. 112.

An Understated Masterpiece

Some people are masters of understatement. They are able to communicate the size, power, or importance of something, not by flapping their arms wildly and loudly piling one hyperbolic adjective on top of another, but by the slight arch of a single eyebrow and the deft choice of a muted phrase. Masters of understatement.

There are, for example, relatives of mine in the South who still describe the American Civil War, a war of immense destructiveness and tragic proportions, by pursing their lips and speaking of "the recent unpleasantness." Masters of understatement.

Several years ago, in one of Hollywood's several grade-B attempts to recreate the world of the Old Testament, there was a scene where emissaries from the Queen of Sheba are sent to visit the court of King Solomon. Before they arrive, however, the wrath of the Lord has been kindled, for various reasons, against Israel, and several catastrophes have been visited upon the people. Cattle have died in the fields from a dreadful pox. Solomon's guards have been struck blind on the city wall, tumbling to gruesome cinematographic deaths. As a finale, a bolt of lightning has ripped from the heavens to destroy the dome of the royal palace. It is at this point that Sheba's agents arrive, and they are greeted by a scepter-bearing guard who looks out of the corners of his eyes and confides, "We've been under something of a strain around here lately." A master of understatement.

The Great Zacchini was, for many years, a feature attraction at countless carnivals and county fairs. He had one stunt, but it was a dramatic one. As the human cannonball, he would be shot from a cannon across a field and into a waiting net. The blast of the cannon would rattle windows for some distance and clouds of sulphurous smoke would drift across the astonished crowds. Near the end of his career, he was asked by a newspaper reporter how it felt to be shot from a cannon nearly every day of his adult life. The Great Zacchini squinted into the sun, scratched his chin, and replied, "Oh, it's about like anything else."

Some people are masters of understatement. Take, for example, the people who were there in the synagogue at Capernaum the day Jesus was the preacher. They made what surely must be one of the great understatements of all time. What happened, according to the Gospel of Mark, was that Jesus showed up at the synagogue on the Sabbath and preached an unusually powerful sermon. Rather than leaving the congregation bewildered by spending his time parsing Hebrew sentences, splitting theological hairs, and quoting fifteen other rabbis, each quoting someone else, Jesus simply looked them in the eye and preached from the heart. Mark tells us that the congregation was "astonished," but that's not the understatement. It was the congregation who made the understatement, and it came after what happened next.

Right at the end of Jesus' sermon, just as people were leaning over to whisper to each other that it would surely be nice to have preaching like that every week, the spell was broken by the appearance of a demon-possessed man squarely in the middle of the congregation. Where he came from, God only knew. Mark doesn't say. Mark just uses one of his favorite words: immediately. "*Immediately* there was in their synagogue," he says, "a man with an unclean spirit," which is Mark's way of sweeping his hand across the literary table, knocking off whatever was on there before and saying, "You think that was something; look at this!"

So the people couldn't waste too much time thinking about that good sermon, because they had an "immediately" on their hands, and, in this particular case, the "immediately" was a raving man in the middle of church shouting vague threats at the young preacher who had just done such a fine job with the sermon.

"I kno-o-o-w who you are," howled something deep within the man. "You're the H-o-o-o-l-y One of God."

"Shut up," said Jesus. "Come out of him!" Things were getting curiouser and curiouser that Sabbath day in Capernaum. The man fell to the synagogue floor, his arms beating wildly at the air, his legs thrashing out so that people moved back to give him a wide circle, froths of foam and strange cries coming out of his mouth. Then the man became strangely calm and lay very still. Slowly he picked himself up off the floor, his face now tranquil, his eyes clear, his voice measured and composed.

Now comes the understatement. The people in the congregation, having witnessed a scene to rival anything in *The Exorcist,* looked around at each other and said, "What is this? A new teaching!" A new *teaching?* If this had happened in any congregation I know, they may have sat for hours in stupified silence, they may have rushed to the altar in sudden repentance, or they may have leapt out of the church windows in terror, but the last thing they would have done was to comment on how this casting out of a demon constituted an innovation in Christian education. A new *teaching?* Indeed.

Perhaps what the folks at Capernaum said strikes us as incongruously understated because of the almost automatic connection we make between teaching and blandness. Ask the average person to picture a teacher and what will come to mind is a portrait of a rather plain woman with her hair pulled back into a bun, an apple on her desk, a sharpened number two pencil in her hand, and a pair of dark-framed spectacles creeping toward the end of her nose. Or maybe it will be an owlish man in a rumpled tweed jacket bringing traffic to a screeching halt as he obliviously crosses the street on a green light, his face buried in a book of Elizabethan sonnets.

Such images are stereotypes, of course, and those of us who are teachers ourselves complain about their inherent unfairness. But the fact is that most of us have spent enough time suffering through endless vocabulary drills, protracted exercises on factoring equations, and tedious lectures on the Code of Hammurabi to know that the word "teaching" is rarely dynamic enough, inspired enough, or exciting enough to embrace anything as overwhelmingly provocative as what happened that day in Capernaum. A new power, a new revelation, a new event, a new charisma perhaps . . . but a new *teaching?* A masterpiece of understatement.

But even though their description of what happened in worship that day seems almost amusingly understated, the congregation at Capernaum may have been on target nonetheless. To call that dramatic event "a new teaching" may have been, when all is said and done, just the right phrase. Consider this classroom experience. It is only one experience, just one classroom, but almost everyone who has spent any time at all in a school has had at least one like it. The place was a high school English class. The subject was modern drama, and the exercise was a class reading of the script of Frank Gilroy's "The Subject Was Roses." The reading moved toward the final scene, one in which a young man named Timmy is leaving home and attempting to say farewell to John, his stubborn and unfeeling father. The readers were dutiful and lifeless. Students glanced at their watches, waiting for the liberation of the bell. A boy and girl in the back of the class exchanged notes. Another boy, bored, looked out the window at the assistant principal making his way toward the building from the parking lot.

Timmy's lines call for him to say to his father that he has had a dream the night before, a dream he has dreamed many times. In the dream he is told that his father is dead, and, when he hears this news, he runs into the street crying. Someone stops him and asks why he is crying, and he says that he is crying because his father is dead and his father never said he loved him. The boy reading Timmy's part faltered on these lines, his voice taking on a strange timbre. The boy lifted his eyes from the script and looked directly at the teacher. "My father has never said that either," he whispered.

Suddenly the class was attentive. An electric silence filled the room. All eyes were on the teacher, who motioned for the reading to continue. The boy looked again at the page and hoarsely read the next line:

Timmy — It's true you never said you love me. But it's also true that I've never said those words to you.

John — I don't know what you're talking about.

Timmy — I say them now . . .

John — I don't know what you're talking about.

Timmy — I love you, Pop . . . I love you.[1]

The teacher was now standing by the boy, his hand gently on the boy's shoulder. As the teacher held the boy close to him, first one member of the class, then another, spoke quietly and thoughtfully of the difficulty and of the healing power of loving another, even when that love cannot be returned. When the students left the class that day, they left neither bored nor merely informed, but changed. What is this? A new teaching?

If the truth be known, we all hunger in our hearts for somebody to teach us something which will transform our lives by its power. We suffer from the separation of event and knowledge. We attend *events,* from soccer matches to cocktail parties, and leave amused but no wiser. We sit at the feet of teachers and gather *knowledge,* from the value of *pi* to the theories of Freud, and we leave informed but unchanged. We yearn to be a part of an event which leads, not to diversion, but to wisdom. We long to know the truth which does not merely set us thinking, but sets us free.

And in the deepest sense possible, that was exactly what happened that day in the synagogue in Capernaum. An event of startling significance happened before the very eyes of the congregation. The demonic powers were subdued. A human life was restored. Jesus was shown to be Lord over all that seeks to spoil and destroy. And the congregation knew that this was not an event merely for the watching. They could not fold their bulletins after the benediction and walk away. This event was not a mere spectacle, but a lasting command. This event contained a truth which made a claim on their lives. Event and wisdom were bonded together that day. What is this? A new teaching!

Christians are always discovering that Jesus Christ is this kind of teacher. He acts powerfully in our lives, giving us overwhelming experiences of grace and love. But warm and exciting religious experience is not the totality of Jesus' impact on our lives. Every action of Christ brings truth, every experience of Christ forms wisdom in our hearts, every encounter carries an enduring claim upon us to live in new ways. Every time we sing "Amazing Grace" we can also sing "This is a new teaching!"

Since New Year's Day 1984, the family of Sam Todd has been looking for him in vain. A seminary student, Sam left a New Year's party in New York City, wandered off into the city streets, and disappeared. The family has been following every lead, tracing every clue. Their sad and futile search has led to hospitals, shelters for the homeless, and morgues. What would one expect the family to feel under these circumstances? Weary despair? Yes. "The irony is that you're hoping to find something terrible that would at least give the comfort of an explanation," said Sam's brother John. One might even expect to find some rugged hope, and that's there, too. But this

90

is a family who has experienced Jesus Christ, and in that experience Jesus has been their teacher. They have learned from him that personal suffering joins us to the suffering of others, and so Sam's father has said:

> *We are a family of faith. We believe in a loving God who knows where Sam is. Sam is in his care, and we are, too. We live in a world where much more awful things happen all the time; where people living under autocratic governments have "disappeared" and we've known several of them personally. [Sam's disappearance] is an awful thing for us, but it's pretty mild compared to that, and this sometimes makes us feel humble*[2]

A family who has lost a son, but who is able, in that experience and through their faith in Jesus Christ, to have compassion on others who suffer. What is this? . . . A new teaching!

Notes

[1] Frank D. Gilroy, *About Those Roses,* and the text of *The Subject Was Roses* (New York: Random House, 1965), p. 209.

[2] From the *New York Times,* January 5, 1985. The account of Sam Todd's family first appeared in Thomas G. Long, "Homiletical Notes for Eastertide," *Journal for Preachers,* Vol. VIII, No. 3 (Easter, 1985) pp. 6-7. This material is used by permission.

Mark 1:29-39

Epiphany 5 (C, L)
Ordinary Time 5 (RC)

A Tempting and Lonely Place

There is nothing more tempting than a lonely place. A lonely place where phones do not ring and loud voices all shouting at once do not compete for our attention. A lonely place where we can hear ourselves think, feel our own calmed breathing, rediscover the inner rhythms which seek in vain to regulate our lives. A lonely place where we can listen to the wind rippling through the trees or, perhaps, to the full and wise sound of stillness. A lonely place free from the cant of television and the condemnation of calendars. A place of tranquil rest and blessed retreat. There is nothing more tempting than a lonely place.

"And in the morning," Mark tells us, "a great while before day, Jesus rose and went out to a lonely place, and there he prayed." (Mark 1:35)

There is nothing more tempting than a lonely place, and most of us search eagerly for such a location. For some of us, the lonely place is actually a *place,* a spot high in the mountains where the air is hushed and the world below seems serene, a rock on the edge of the ocean where we can lose our thoughts among the restless waves and the vast gray depths, or even a private spot near our home where we can walk to be alone beneath the starry night sky.

For others of us, we must be content with a lonely place which is really a *time.* A little solitude in the car between sales

appointments, a last cup of morning coffee with only the ac-
companiment of a quietly humming refrigerator, or a few
minutes watching the fire die in the fireplace, the house silent
after all others have gone to bed.

There is nothing more tempting than a lonely place. We
all seek such places, guard them, and cherish them. "And in
the morning a great while before day, Jesus rose and went out
to a lonely place, and there he prayed."

Occasionally, in my preaching classes, I ask my students
to preach a sermon from any text of their choice from the first
chapter of Mark. There are many rich passages to be found
there: the preaching of John the Baptizer, the baptism of
Jesus, the beginning of Jesus' ministry, the first call of the
disciples, the healing of a leper. All of these stories, and more,
are there in Mark's opening chapter, and yet most of the students do not select any of these passages. Pressed by exams
and papers, crowded by the demands of families and weekend
jobs, feeling the pull of too much work and too many demands,
most of them are irresistibly drawn to the seductive tranquility
of this story about Jesus rising early in the morning to go to
a lonely place. The sermons they create are as predictable as
they are passionate: Jesus had spent the previous day, they
say, in a fever pitch of ministry, preaching in the synagogue,
healing the sick and demon-possessed, and now, in a moment
of needed retreat, he rises early in the morning to go to a lonely
place to pray. Just so, they go on to claim, we, too, need times
of quiet reflection and serene prayer lest the busy world crowd
out the voice of God. As the old hymn goes, "There is a place
of quiet rest, near to the heart of God." These sermons, like
most sermons, say at least as much about the preachers as they
do about the hearers — ministers desperately in need of a lonely
place. There is nothing more tempting than a lonely place.

But these sermons miss something important about the
character of the lonely place. Mark wants us to know that,
in a way we have perhaps not imagined, there is indeed nothing
more tempting than a lonely place, because the "lonely place,"

when it is truly a place of coming to grips with what is most urgent about life and important about ourselves, is finally not a place of calm, but of temptation. The lonely place is not a placid retreat, but a place of crisis and decision.

The word which is translated "lonely place" in our story is *heramos,* and "lonely place" is too gentle a translation of this word, because it hints at untroubled tranquility, a fall afternoon in peaceful woods walking across a carpet of golden leaves. A better rendering of this word is "wilderness," a place filled with danger, where the spirits lurk and temptation stalks. Mark uses this word *heramos* many times in his opening chapter, and it always carries the meaning of a place where crucial and risky decisions are being made. It is out in the *heramos* that John the Baptizer fills the air with a cry for repentance. John is, in Isaiah's words, the "voice of one crying in the *heramos.* Jesus is driven by the Spirit into the *heramos* to be tempted, and the *heramos* is inhabited both by angels and wild beasts. The *heramos* is the place where God's will is made clear and where the demand for obedience becomes urgent. It is also the place where the temptation to disobey is felt most powerfully. The *heramos* is a holy place, alive with the presence of God. The *heramos* is a dangerous place, the atmosphere charged with the possibility of betrayal. And the *heramos* is the place where Jesus went that morning to pray. There is nothing more tempting than a lonely place.

And the temptation came. In the lonely place, while Jesus was at prayer, the temptation came . . . in a surprising form. Peter and those with him found Jesus and said, "Everyone is searching for you." Just that. Like most real temptations, this one hardly seems like a temptation, but in this apparently innocent sentence there was a deep enticement to betrayal. "Everyone is searching for you," said Peter. In other words, come back. Come back to Capernaum and stay, stay where you healed the sick and astonished people with your preaching. People love and admire you there. Come back. Let your ministry end where it began. Become Capernaum's local wonder worker, their private priest. Everyone is searching for you. Come back and stay.

There was Jesus in the *heramos,* the lonely place, with two paths leading out. One path led back to Capernaum and a life of comfortable popularity. The other path led on to Golgotha and a costly sacrifice. One path led to a place where all were crying, "Hosanna." The other path led to a place where all would cry, "Crucify him." The lonely place was no place of serene reflection; it was a place of momentous decision, the Kingdom of Self-interest versus the Kingdom of God. Facing the tempter again, Jesus decided: "Let us go on to the next towns, that I may preach there also; for that is why I came out." (Mark 1:38)

As Henri Nouwen has stated it:

> . . . *the secret of Jesus' ministry is hidden in that lonely place where he went to pray . . .*
>
> *In the lonely place Jesus finds the courage to follow God's will and not his own; to speak God's words and not his own; to do God's work and not his own.*[1]

When we choose to follow Jesus there are lonely places for us, too. Not the gentle lonely places of retreat from the pressures of life, but the wilderness places and times when, in the midst of crisis or simply heightened awareness, we must choose between our own will and God's, between our own words and God's, between our own work and God's. There is nothing more tempting than a lonely place.

Sometimes the lonely wilderness is a place of tumult, a place we would not go unless we had been driven there. A marriage falls apart, a job is lost, a loved one suffers in pain, one we had trusted betrays us. These are lonely places, and their perils are all too clear. Sometimes it seems to us that the holy thing to do in such places, the "godly" choice to make, is to suffer in silence. "It is God's will," we tell ourselves, or "God would not place on us more than we can bear." These seem to be the faithful options, something of a righteous "Que Sera," but we must be careful. Sometimes the thing which appears most holy and sacrificial — for example, going back to live and minister among the many needy people in Capernaum — is the very temptation God would have us avoid.

In Elie Wiesel's *The Town Beyond the Wall,* there is a rebellious character who has profoundly experienced the lonely place of human suffering and who chooses not to bear this in silence. He loudly laments, crying angrily to God that his fate is unjust, indeed, that God is unjust. It would seem that he had fallen into the snare of temptation, but he confesses:

> *I want to blaspheme, and I can't quite manage it. I go up against [God], I shake my fist, I froth with rage, but it's still a way of telling Him that He's there . . . that denial itself is an offering to His grandeur. The shout becomes a prayer in spite of me.*[2]

Sometimes, when the lonely place is a place of great disturbance, it evokes our rage against God, clarifies how seriously we take God's power and presence and, thereby, brings us even closer to God. "The shout becomes a prayer in spite of me."

Most of the time, though, our wilderness places are not nearly so turbulent as that. They are the quieter and more gentle places, the places close to home and ordinary routine, the spaces between the activities of our lives, where we nonetheless make the crucial decisions of our lives.

The late Carlyle Marney was once asked where the Garden of Eden was located. "Two fifteen Elm Street, Knoxville, Tennessee," replied Marney. The questioner found that incredulous and challenged Marney with the notion that the Garden of Eden was somewhere in Asia. Marney said that you couldn't prove that by him, because it was at Two fifteen Elm Street that, as a boy, he had stolen some money from his mother's purse and gone to the store and spent it on candy. When he returned he was so ashamed he hid in the closet. "It was there [my mama] found me," he said, "and asked, 'Where are you? Why are you hiding? What have you done?' '' The Garden of Eden, the place of temptation, the "lonely place" was, for Marney, on Elm Street.[3]

The lonely place, the place of temptation and decision, the place where we decide to follow God's call or our own noses, can be a breakfast table or a closet, a moment of insight reading a novel or an argument with someone we love, in the morning or at night, when we are tired or when we are refreshed, in the singing of a hymn or in the sighing of a prayer, in the second act of a play or even . . . in the middle of a sermon.

The Methodist pastor and chaplain William Willimon once received an agitated telephone call on a Sunday evening from a parishioner in his church. He said that his daughter Anne had just decided to drop out of pharmacy school. Anne had been home for the weekend. In fact she had worshiped with her mother and father that morning, and the news of her leaving school had caught them totally by surprise. Willimon asked why Anne was doing such a thing, but the father was uncertain. What he mainly wanted was for Willimon to call his daughter and "talk some sense into her."

Willimon called Anne and reminded her of the many hours she had already put into pharmaceutical training and of her many academic achievements, all of which she now seemed to be willing to throw away. "How in the world did you come to this decision?" Willimon asked.

"Well," she said, "it was your sermon yesterday that started me thinking." She went on to describe her own experience of a lonely place. She admitted that she was in pharmacy school to earn a good living and to meet her own self-defined needs. Willimon's sermon had emphasized the call of God which comes to all of us, that God has something important for all of us to do. The sermon had caused Anne to remember the satisfying summer she had spent teaching in the church literacy program among migrant workers, a time when she genuinely felt as though she was serving God. She told Willimon that, after his sermon, she had decided to leave school and to give her life to helping those people. "There was a long silence on my end of the telephone," wrote Willimon. " 'Now look Anne,' I said at last, 'I was just preaching.' "[4]

Even a sermon can be a lonely place, a place of temptation, a place of decision, a place of peril . . . and a place of holiness. A lonely place is where we decide whether we shall go where we have been sent by Cod, or go where "the devil may care." Jesus chose to go where he was sent, "to the other towns," and, we must never forget that because he did, he came to our town to minister, too. And he is there even now, in our lonely places, beckoning us, if we will, to follow.

Notes

[1] Henri J. M. Nouwen, *Out of Solitude: Three Meditations on the Christian Life* (Notre Dame, Indiana: Ave Maria Press, 1974), p. 14

[2] Elie Wiesel, *The Town Beyond the Wall,* as quoted in Robert McAfee Brown, *Creative Dislocations: The Movement of Grace* (Nashville: Abingdon Press, 1980), p. 90.

[3] The story about Carlyle Marney is told in William H. Willimon, *Sighing for Eden: Sin, Evil, and the Christian Faith* (Nashville: Abingdon Press, 1985), p. 24.

[4] William H. Willimon, *What's Right With the Church* (San Francisco: Harper and Row Publishers, 1985), pp. 112-3.

Living in the Future Present

Back to the Future is a highly imaginative motion picture which prospered at the box office several years ago. The film features a madcap scientist who perfects a machine capable of achieving the human dream of traveling through time. A teenaged boy uses the machine to journey to his hometown as it was in the 1950s, before the boy was born. What happens in the movie from that point on is, of course, ludicrously good fun. The boy meets his parents and discovers what they were like in their awkward teenage years. He dazzles the populace with the unknown sport of skateboarding, and he even manages to introduce Chuck Berry to the throbbing guitar licks of the as-yet-unwritten "Johnny B. Goode." Signs of 50's quaintness abound, from soda bottles whose caps will *not* twist off to a service station with a platoon of crisply uniformed attendants who swarm each car to check the oil, clean the windshield, and sweep off the floor mats.

For all of its warm frivolity, however, this movie does ponder one serious theme: how possessing knowledge of the future would create an awesome responsibility in the present. Before moving back into time, the boy has been warned not to attempt to alter the future in any way. Indeed, as the plot unfolds, the boy has to work vigorously to insure that the future he has already seen and lived does in fact develop. His mother and father, for example, are having difficulty, as teenagers, developing a romantic relationship, and the boy has to employ every ounce of his inventiveness to insure that the conditions are created which will lead to their mutual attraction, eventual marriage, and, paradoxically, the boy's own birth. Because the boy knows the future, he bears its burden and is compelled to work for its fulfillment.

The movie is playful, but the insight is a serious one. Knowledge of the future creates momentous responsibility in the present. Imagine a physician checking the lab reports one more time, to find that they say the same thing as before: the disease has spread beyond the bounds of containment. For one moment in time the physician is the one person in the world who knows what the future holds for this patient, that his life is now numbered in days. Although some might think this knowledge would lessen the physician's responsibility, for the patient is now outside the limits of her skill and of medicine's power, the physician knows otherwise. As she enters the patient's room, and the patient and his family look toward her, wonderingly, hopefully, she is deeply aware that the awful truth she knows about the future has placed the heaviest responsibility of all upon her shoulders.

Or think of an executive in a large firm. He knows that in a matter of weeks his company will be purchased by a larger corporation. One result, among others, will be a sharp rise in the value of his company's stock. Wall Street does not know this yet, but *he* does. In his Saturday golf match, one of his partners casually mentions that he is about to start a college investment program for his two small children. He asks the others what sort of investment thay would suggest — savings bonds? real estate? stocks? At that moment the executive feels the weight of future knowledge. Should he tell this man about the upcoming merger? His friend is no market sharpie seeking insider information; he is a father trying to stretch some savings into a decent education for his children. On the other hand, it *is* illegal to reveal this privileged information, and the executive finally decides the struggle in favor of silence and the law. For a few minutes, though, he felt the burden which comes when one knows the future.

I once had the privilege of having a private conversation with a man who was well-known for his books and lectures on human relationships. He was an elderly man, and the kind of open spirit who welcomed questions on any subject, so I felt brave enough to ask him what was the main change that aging had brought to his life. He thought for a bit, then replied, "I view everything from the point of view of my death." At first his answer struck me as strange, even morbid. But as he continued to speak, I realized that his response was full, not of dread, but of wisdom. He now possessed the maturity to acknowledge what younger people often avoid and deny: he was mortal. He grasped existentially the truth that he would die, and his remaining days were shaped by that coming event into a time both precious and urgent. Instead of blithely crossing off the blocks on the calendar, his knowledge of the future had placed upon him the responsibility of making the remaining time matter. He had begun, to use the language of the Psalmist, "to number his days" instead of just counting them.

The transfiguration of Jesus is also a glimpse into the future. It is not just *a* glimpse into *any* future; it is a clear vision of the ultimate future, God's future, and, as such, it creates for all disciples of Jesus the most awesome responsibility human beings can be given. The event occurs in the middle of Jesus' ministry, indeed, almost literally in the middle of Mark's gospel. The account is a strange ona, filled with symbolism. Peter, James, and John are apart with Jesus on a high mountain, the symbolic place of revelation. Jesus garments begin to shine with a brilliant whiteness, the sign of God's presence, the *Shekinah*. Jesus converses with the great figures Moses and Elijah, and then, suddenly, there is only Jesus, and the voice of God, which spoke at Jesus' baptism, again declaring him to be the "Son of God."

Mark tells us that, in the middle of this experience, Peter said to Jesus, "Master, it is well that we are here; let us make three booths, one for you, and one for Moses, and one for

Elijah.'' Sometimes we say that what Peter wanted to do was to preserve the moment, to freeze time at the peak of this mountaintop experience. Perhaps so, but there is more to it than that. The commentator David Nineham has pointed out that Peter's suggestion of building booths was itself a recognition that he was face-to-face with the future. The Jewish Feast of Booths had come to mean, not only a remembrance of the days when God dwelled with his people in tents in the wilderness, but also a looking forward to the day when God and his people, people of all nations, would again "tabernacle" together. Peter looked at the shining appearance of the glorified Jesus in the company of Moses and Elijah, and he assumed that this long-expected day had finally come. The future had arrived. "Let us build the booths," he said.[1]

But Peter was mistaken. The future had been seen, but it had not yet fully come The transfiguration occurs in the *middle* of Jesus' ministry. There was still ahead a journey into the valley full of demons to be cast out, disputes to be settled, rejection to be faced, burdens to be borne, suffering to be endured, and a cross to be carried. The future had been seen, and now it shaped the present with urgent responsibility.

Mark also tells us that Peter said what he did about the booths because he was *afraid,* and well he should have been. People who have seen the future and who know what it holds are compelled to live differently in the present. They are now accountable to that future, and they can no longer rock along in life whistling "I'il take tomorrow as it comes." They *know* what tomorrow holds, and they must live each present day in the sure knowledge of what is to be. That day on the mountain Peter saw into the future, and what he saw was that this Jesus is the Lord of all time. Now he must go back to a valley full of illness, danger, and suffering with the awareness that, after what he had seen, serving any other than this Lord would be betrayal. Small wonder he wanted to bypass all of this and hasten the arrival of the future. Small wonder he wanted to go ahead and make the *booths* now. Small wonder he was afraid.

One day, when my daughter was a little girl, she was dancing playfully in our living room. I was on the couch trying to read the newspaper, but her whirling motion captured my attention. I watched her spin, her arms spread wide and her hair tossing as she twirled across the room. Suddenly the way her mouth was fixed, the manner in which her hair fell across her cheeks, and the play of sunlight through the curtains on her face created an unusual effect. For one instant she looked not five years old, but twenty-five. There was a single fixed-frame in her motion when I saw her, not as a child, but as the grown-up woman she would become. Then she turned, the light changed, her face broke into a grin, and she was a child again. But I had seen what I had seen, and there was no escaping it. It was a wonderful moment, and a frightening one as well. Wonderful because I had seen my daughter as a mature woman. Frightening because I anticipated what it would take to live toward that day. She would not be a child forever, and I must be willing to relinquish that. Every present moment must now be arched toward that future when I would no longer be her protector and guide in the old and familiar ways. Every experience in the present must nurture the adulthood already growing within her.

In Jesus Christ we have seen what God's future is like, and Mark rightfully calls that the "good news." But Mark also preserves the fearful side of that truth as well. We are now responsible to the future we have seen. We must live today in the light of that tomorrow, even if that means scorn, sacrifice, and suffering. Peter saw the future that day on the mountain of transfiguration, and he was afraid. Some women saw the future that first Easter Day at the tomb, and Mark tells us that they, too, were afraid. (Mark 16:8)

Lutheran Pastor Richard John Neuhaus once described Christian people as ambassadors of a disputed sovereignty who have arrived at court too soon. We have seen the future in which Jesus is Lord, and we are called to serve him in a time when his Lordship is hidden and seems in doubt. We know that the future belongs to the Prince of Peace, and so we work for peace in a war-torn age. We know that one day justice will roll down like waters, and we work today for that justice, even though such labor is costly. We have seen the risen Christ, and we know that in him the image of aod in humanity has been restored. Therefore, we work today for the poor, the outcast, and all others denied dignity in our age.

It is a fearsome responsibility to have seen the future, but the future we have seen is God's future, and it is sure. One day Peter's wish will be fulfilled, and the booths will be built. "In that day," says John the Evangelist . . .

> . . . *God will dwell with them and they shall be*
> *his people,*
> *and God himself will be with them;*
> *He will wipe away every tear from their eyes,*
> *and death shall be no more,*
> *neither shall there be mourning, nor crying,*
> *nor pain anymore,*
> *for the former things have passed away.*

(Revelation 21:3-4)

Then our fearful hearts, and Peter's, too, will know one more truth. God's future is a time of perfect love, and perfect love casts out all fear.

Notes

1 D. E. Nineham, *Saint Mark* [The Pelican New Testament Commentaries] (New York: Penguin Books, 1963), pp. 236-7.

When Nothing Can Be Done

"I'm sorry, nothing can be done." There are probably no more terrible words than these. They mark the end of labor, the end of possibility, the end of hope.

The family holds vigil in the surgical waiting room. The dated magazines on the table have been read and re-read. The wall clock moves in slow motion, and the family waits. A dark spot on an X-ray demanded attention. "We just don't know," the surgeon had said. "We'll have to go in and check." Now he appears, a loosened surgical mask around his neck, his face lined with concern. "I'm sorry," he begins, "there's nothing we can do."

A woman sits before a desk in a glass cubicle in the corner of a large room full of similar desks. She has spent the day in front of these desks, passed from one clerk to the next. She has been ignored and condescended to, but she has been persistent, and now she is speaking earnestly to the department head in charge of county social services. Her husband is dead, she tells him. She lost her job some time ago in a lay-off at the plant, bills are long overdue, and now the sheriff's deputy has delivered a foreclosure notice on her small house. The man thumbs through her file, picks up his phone and speaks softly to someone at the other end. He cradles the receiver, knits his fingers together and says, "I'm sorry. Nothing can be done."

There are probably no more terrible words than these. Until they are spoken, there may be pain, but there is always hope.

Even when a struggle is mounted against overwhelming odds, there is at least the dignity of doing something, anything, about one's circumstances. But "nothing can be done" ends the meaningfulness of the struggle and destroys what remains of dignity. "All hope abandon, ye who enter here," were the words Dante imagined over the final portals of Hell. "Nothing can be done."

To be a leper in New Testament times was to live constantly under the motto, "Nothing can be done." The disease transformed its victims into loathsome, disfigured creatures, shunned by all. It was hopelessly incurable, and even the person's own body seemed to turn on itself. Journalist Philip Yancey reports that modern-day visitors to leper colonies in rural villages in Africa and Asia have seen the sufferers reach into pots of boiling water to recover the vegetables cooking there. They feel no pain at all, even though the scalding water raises blisters on the flesh and destroys tissue. Even the body's pain system, which normally warns of danger, abandons this dreaded disease.[1]

Make no mistake about it. When Jesus encountered the leper that day in Galilee he was face-to-face with the most hopeless and untouchable of all people. Physically disgusting, unwelcome at worship, the leper was also beyond the care even of Holy Scripture. As New Testament scholar D.E. Nineham has stated it, "The Law could do nothing for the leper; it could only protect the rest of the community against him."[2] Even the community of faith had to wring its hands and say, "I'm sorry. Nothing can be done."

All of which makes what the leper said to Jesus absolutely astonishing. "If you will," he said, "you can make me clean." Faith begins at the outer limits of human resources. Perhaps that is why we American Christians often find our faith weak and our religious expression trivial when contrasted with the vibrant discipleship of Christians around the world who live in places of persecution. Where there are still plots to be hatched, angles to be pursued, human stratagems to be tried, faith struggles to survive. The leper was cut out of all the plots. He had no angles, possessed no stratagems. All he had was leprosy . . . and the damning verdict ringing in his ears, "I'm sorry. Nothing can be done." Here at the boundary of human hope, one's choices are narrowed to two: Be resigned to fate or reach toward the mystery of grace beyond all hoping.

The leper refused to accept the verdict of fate. He reached — reached out toward the mystery of grace he discerned in this man Jesus. His was an amazing profession of faith: "If you will, you can make me clean."

At the cold and forlorn memorial which was once the Dachau death camp, there are signs all around of that time when hatred filled the world. There are the rough barracks where Jews and the other prisoners were cruelly housed. There are whips and other instruments of torture in the museum, and there are, of course, the gas chambers and the ovens. There is also something else. At one end of the camp, there stand three chapels, one Protestant, one Roman Catholic, and one Jewish. At the opposite end of the camp is a monument which reads, "Never again." Now there is nothing in human history which warrants that statement. Humanity has manifested uncontrolled evil before, and even now there are places where the savagery present at Dachau is yet at work. If the chapels and the monument point only to the potential for goodness in the human heart, then they are mocked by history. The monument should read, "We're sorry. Nothing can be done." But, of course, these symbols point beyond the tragic circumstances of human evil. They express a hope beyond all normal human hoping, a hope that there is at work in the world a power which will finally topple evil from its invincible throne.

The jury was in. All had testified against the leper: family, respected members of the community, even his ministers. The verdict? "We're sorry. Nothing can be done." Next case. But, in faith, the leper refused to accept the verdict, appealed to the court of last resort, reached toward the mystery of grace in Jesus. "If you will, you can make me clean."

In Tillie Olsen's moving story "I Stand Here Ironing," she pictures an anxious and impoverished mother standing at the ironing board and thinking about her troubled nineteen-year-old daughter, Emily. A note has come from the school asking her to come in to discuss Emily's problems, and this starts her mother remembering Emily's childhood. Emily was a beautiful baby, a miracle, remembers her mother, but when she was eight months old her father abandoned the family, and Emily had to be left during the day with a woman downstairs "to whom she was no miracle at all." Then, as economic hardship increased, Emily was left in the kind of nursery school which is only a "parking place" for children. Her mother did not know then the pain that was in that place for Emily, but, as she irons and reflects, she admits that knowledge could not have made a difference. She had to hold a job, and the nursery school was the only place for Emily.

Emily was a thin girl, and she was dark and foreign-looking in a time when little girls were supposed to be blond and plump and cute. She was a "slow learner" in a world where quickness and glibness are valued. She was a child, not of proud love, but anxious love. And now, a note has come from school, but Emily's mother knows that too much has happened to Emily for there to be any real help for her at the school. As she moves the iron back and forth across the ironing board, thinking of the isolation and poverty and rejection which have been Emily's inheritance, she cries to herself, and to whatever power of mercy there may be beyond herself:

> She has much to her and probably little will come of it. Let her be . . . Only help her to know — help make it so there is cause to know — that she is more than this dress on the ironing board, helpless before the iron.[3]

Emily is a modern day leper, one about whom her culture has sadly shaken its head and said, "I'm sorry. The die has been cast. The scars are too deep. Nothing can be done." And yet, in her mother's desperate cry there is a hope beyond all

108

hoping, an appeal to the last resort of grace. "Help her to know," she prays, "that she is more than this dress on the ironing board, helpless . . ."

"If you will," said the leper to Jesus, "you can heal me." And Jesus was moved with strong compassion. The One who was, and is, and ever will be the "help of the helpless" was deeply moved, and, stretching out his grace-filled hand, he touched the untouchable leper. "I will," he said. "Be clean." The sad and condemning "nothing can be done" was abolished by the merciful word, "I will." New Testament scholar R. H. Lightfoot has suggested that the best commentary on this event can be found in Romans 8:3: "God has done what the law . . . could not do: sending his own Son . . ."[4]

The essayist Loren Eiseley once spent some time on the coast of Costabel. In the dark hours before morning, the beaches there are littered with the barely-living debris of creatures thrown onto the sand by the passionless tides. Flashlights and lanterns bob along the beach as shell and starfish collectors greedily seize what the sea has given them. One night, Eiseley noticed a lone figure on the beach stooping to pick up some object and then flinging it far out into the sea. Eiseley went over to this man and discovered that what he had thrown was a starfish, still alive. "It may live," he said, "if the offshore pull is strong enough. The stars throw well. One can help them." As Eiseley left the man, he saw him toss another starfish back into the sea. Viewing this experience as a parable, Eiseley wrote:

Somewhere, my thought persisted, there is a hurler of stars, and he walks, because he chooses, always in desolation, but not in defeat.[5]

"If you will," said the desolate and hopeless leper, "you can make me clean."

"I will," said Jesus, and stretching out his hand, Jesus grasped the leper with tender mercy and flung him far into the deep and healing waters of the sea of grace.

109

Notes

[1] Philip Yancey, *Open Windows* (Nashville: Thomas Nelson Publishers, 1985), p. 161.

[2] D. E. Nineham, *Saint Mark* [The Pelican New Testament Commentaries] (New York: Penguin Books, 1963), p. 86.

[3] Tillie Olsen, "I Stand Here Ironing" in *Tell Me A Riddle* (New York: Dell Books, 1971), pp. 20-21.

[4] R. H. Lightfoot, *The Gospel Message of Saint Mark* (London: Oxford University Press, 1950), p. 26.

[5] Loren Eiseley, *The Unexpected Universe* (New York: Harcourt, Brace and World, 1969), p. 91.